THE GARDENS OF ULF NORDFJELL

THE GARDENS OF ULF NORDFJELL

PHOTOGRAPHY
JASON INGRAM

PHOTOGRAPHY OF EKHOLMSNÄS MANOR
LISEN STIBECK

FOREWORD
ANNIE GATTI

MERRELL
LONDON • NEW YORK

CONTENTS

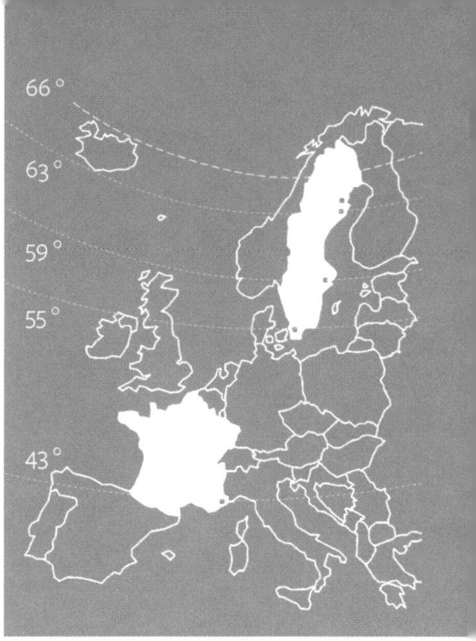

Preface: The Dream of a Garden

Where do our dreams come from? And what can we learn from comparing gardens at different latitudes?

These are two of the questions I have chosen to focus on in this book, which is based on my roughly forty years of experience as a landscape architect. The book follows the development of a number of gardens and parks, located from just beneath the Arctic Circle to the French Riviera. It outlines how inspiration is provided by the geographical location, but also by the climate change that is occurring at an increasing rate. It is important for me that any design should fit both place and climate. Here you will encounter everything from contrasting winter silhouettes in Scandinavia, and bright spring flowers followed by light summer nights, to abundant summer flowers and warm, dark nights on the Riviera.

I have tried to convey my love and respect for nature, and my experience of creating planting combinations of varying scales. My interest in merging nature and horticulture with architecture and design – and in the process itself, creating networks of skills at all stages – finds fresh expression in every new project.

Climate and the seasons

In this book I want to focus on how parks and gardens relate to the climate and the seasons. In my world, where classical ideals and the bounty of nature meet, the expression and embodiment of time are constantly changing, and this is enhanced by the cycle of the seasons. Added to this is the climate change of our age, which is affecting parks and gardens in both the short and the long term. Whether in Sweden or further afield, we all have in common this changing climate, which has both positive and negative consequences.

How is the choice of plants influenced by climate change in the form of increased wind and rain throughout the year, and hot, early summers on the Riviera? And in Sweden, where rainy winters and an absence of snow lead to increasing amounts of ice in our gardens?

It isn't possible to present a comprehensive view of these complex subjects, but through a selection of my work I hope to show a number of examples based on experience. Don't let yourself be blinded by their grandeur, but see them as guidance, bearing in mind that this experience can be applied to all gardens, big and small.

The process

For me, landscape architecture is about teamwork, from initial concept to construction, and also in following the development of each project after its completion. I hope to entice you into following me on some of these journeys, which I find remarkable. Every journey starts with a client, whether public or private. For me, the conditions and analysis of the site form the basis for the sketches that follow. In the early stages of this sketching, I am happiest out in the country, at Forsstugan, my cabin by the rapids (see pages 11–35). There, nature and the changing seasons give me the energy to harness the facts and the time to sketch my ideas.

My gardens and parks reflect my design language, but are also portraits of the contemporary world – just as gardens and parks always have been. Nature is my greatest inspiration and driving force. I love springtime in the country, and never cease to be enchanted by the light playing on the water of the rapids and the sound of the spring birds.

The conceptual development of each project is a process that must be allowed to take time, and that requires input from various sources. At the next stage, ideas and thoughts are developed and refined into something more concrete so that they begin to come to life. As part of this work, and to make the project achievable and sustainable over time, the skills of various experts are required.

The resulting designs and outlines form the basis of the construction process that follows. In the public arena, to avoid extra expense, it is important that anything not in the design doesn't get built. In a private garden, the process looks rather different. Here, collaboration can be more fluid, and the dialogue with the client continues, even during construction.

I am convinced that knowledge, experience and personal chemistry are preconditions for fruitful dialogue, and to make the project enjoyable. Good collaboration allows greater freedom to try new ideas, new solutions, and different lighting and materials once work has started. My way of working combines experience with the latest techniques to create sustainable parks and gardens that develop positively over time, and to make their care and maintenance easier. There is a constant shortage of trained and experienced maintenance staff, and over the years it has been very important to me to support this important profession. Close collaboration with construction and maintenance teams in Sweden and the United Kingdom and on the French Riviera has always been and remains a source of knowledge and joy for me, and essential for good results.

The photographers

Sharing my work with readers requires the work of photographers with a sensitive eye for the architecture of the garden. Jason Ingram, an internationally renowned garden photographer, has photographed selected gardens and parks with a focus on the changing seasons – from the pale northern light to the warm illumination of the Mediterranean. The Covid-19 pandemic disrupted this work, and that is evident in some of the pictures in terms of the growth and maturity of the gardens.

Lisen Stibeck, a Stockholm photographer and owner of two of the gardens featured, has photographed Ekholmsnäs Manor. Yanan Li has also contributed a number of photographs to the book. Their pictures show how differently we can see a garden.

Ulf Nordfjell, June 2024

Foreword

The very first time I saw a garden designed by Sweden's pre-eminent landscape architect, Ulf Nordfjell, was in 2007, when he presented the first of three gold-medal Chelsea Flower Show gardens. I was captivated by the elegance of his 'Tribute to Carl Linnaeus' garden, by the impeccable arrangement of cool native planting within a strong framework of granite, timber and steel elements.

I have since had the privilege of visiting several private gardens designed by Ulf, including his own beloved riverside garden below the Arctic Circle, which lies buried under snow for five months of the year, and I have been struck by how skilfully he connects them to the surrounding landscapes. I have also seen how, thanks to his encyclopedic knowledge of plants and the conditions they require in order to thrive, the gardens sing in all seasons, starting in the spring with explosions of colour and texture.

This book offers an immersion, both in words and images, into Ulf Nordfjell's recent work in Sweden and the South of France. The gardens and parks, created in the decade from 2010 to 2020, vary in scale and setting, from city courtyard to historic country estate, but they share the designer's thoughtful response to the effects of climate change. He shows how, by adapting planting palettes and selecting new species, by improving soils and installing watering schemes, his gardens – and ours – can withstand extremes. Boosting biodiversity through plant choice is another shared aspect, as is the designer's signature use of trees and shrubs, often in fastigiate, pleached or multi-stem forms, to provide structure, and his restraint in the chosen materials and extent of hard landscaping.

These are restful places, rigorously designed but relaxed in effect. In the hands of this master of the art of landscape architecture and garden design, they are also places that have been designed to endure.

Annie Gatti

The Cabin by the Rapids

A garden by a Norrland river

This garden, our family's paradise, lies inland from the Gulf of Bothnia, in a sub-Arctic climate that often gives cold, dry winters with heavy snow, and warm, sunny – but short – summers.

When the snow withdraws in April, nature is on standby; as soon as the wild willow is in bloom, the first of the garden's snowdrops appear. The budding flowers are hastened by the light nights. In May crocus and blue and white scilla, followed by blue and white wood anemones, other bulbs and pulmonaria, fill the garden with a longed-for feeling of spring. The birds return, and bees and butterflies awaken, making nature vibrate with life.

Where summers are short

As the soil warms up, the plants get going. Perennials rise from the ground and the shoots of the shuttlecock fern unfurl to dizzying heights. It is a short but wonderful time that, at a furious pace, gives us back everything we have missed, and even though I have experienced this transformation every year of my life, I am just as enchanted every spring. The seasons seem to overlap; for instance, it isn't unusual for tulips to linger until midsummer, as a delightful complement to the bright greenery of perennials. Tulips add colours that perennials rarely offer, and the relationship between late-flowering bulbs and perennials gives the garden its special atmosphere. Sometimes summer flowers are early enough to keep the tulips company, which makes a spectacular impression – much like at the Chelsea Flower Show. There you often see plant combinations that would never normally flower at the same time, but here in the far north it isn't a show, it's for real!

These garden combinations are made possible by the light summer nights, when the martagon lilies and daylilies are in bloom at the same time as peonies and poppies. And, because the nights are relatively cool, the flowers remain fresh for longer. In August, as the nights lengthen, such plants as sweet peas and dahlias thrive, as well as late summer perennials, such as phlox and veronicastrum.

At that time of year there is a generous harvest of summer flowers, vegetables and currants. By contrast, late-flowering perennials

Dawn over the Öre River.

A great part of the garden consists of preserved natural areas, which we love, and which we look after to stop them from becoming overgrown. At the same time, we preserve the view of the river landscape. Here pines and firs grow among spring-flowering blueberry and lingonberry, and autumn heather. These are all valuable secondary plants, but the highlight of the season is the heather in August.

don't have time to bloom before the frosts return. The magic of the far north is this brief, rich period when everything is here and now.

In September, when the fiery colours of autumn make their entrance, everything happens as quickly as the arrival of spring. Cool nights combined with warm days provide an abundance of colour both in the garden and out in nature. This short season is intense, and by the end of October, when the first tentative snow falls, we and the garden are ready for our winter rest.

Christmases always used to be white, with reliable snow cover year after year, but this is no longer the case. These days one winter can bring copious snow, and the next merely a dusting that melts during the day and forms thick layers of ice at night. It is this ice that causes problems for the perennials, above all, and we really aren't used to it.

The changes of season happen suddenly, and just as quickly as winter comes to an end, our enthusiasm for the garden awakens again.

New life in our beloved garden

Everything has its time. After two large exhibition gardens at the RHS Chelsea Flower Show in 2007 and 2009, with gold medals and Best in Show in the bag, my adrenalin was high and my happiness knew no limits. Once I was back home, a long-standing dream of taking a firm grip on our tired garden was awakened. My husband, Leif, and I started to fantasize about a design for the future together.

The old design, with its roots in my childhood, had – as so often happens – developed gradually over the years, with additions and changes that perhaps didn't lead anywhere. The planting had developed and been replaced piecemeal, and some of the beds had been fed with so much compost that they had grown to awkward heights. The seating areas were too small, and the distribution of sun and shade no longer suited our needs. We decided to embark on a major rebuild – what could be more fun than a new, joint gardening project at home?

In this newly awakened rush of joy, we considered tearing out most of the garden and starting again from scratch. In the spring of 2010 our ideas took shape and, excited by this new

adventure, and with a large number of helping hands and mechanical aids, we set to work. The desire to create was great, as was our ambition to incorporate all the ecological experience we had accumulated over the years.

There are probably many of us who have used our gardens as a place for plant collections, without any thought for consistency or composition. Such a collection is difficult to value, since it has many meanings that have nothing to do with the art of gardening. For us it was important to replant the perennials that my mother had added over the years, many of them local cultivars that had been in the garden for more than sixty years. But it was also time for change, and that cast a different light on things: now this was going to be *our* garden.

New structure, in harmony with nature

Once we had made the decision, there was a euphoric excitement about changing the structures and beds, and bringing in new additions, such as greenhouses and a longed-for orangery.

The garden is surrounded by tall pines, which give us a sheltered situation, a supply of wild blueberries and lingonberries, and a wealth of bird and insect life. Our plan was to tighten up the architecture of the garden and make better use of the conditions of the site, without

Scented peonies (*Paeonia lactiflora* 'Duchesse de Nemours' and the single form 'White Wings') and bowman's root (*Gillenia trifoliata*) are plants that have stood the test of time, seen here with flowering hostas with white-edged leaves (*Hosta* 'Patriot'), violas, red-leaved spurge (*Euphorbia dulcis* 'Chameleon') and the annual white laceflower (*Orlaya grandiflora*). In the background is the giant bellflower (*Campanula latifolia* var. *macrantha* 'Alba') in bud and the serrated foliage of goatsbeard (*Aruncus dioicus* 'Kneiffi'). Towards the fence is the Manchurian walnut, and on the fence alpine clematis (*Clematis alpina*). The blue-tinted grass is feather reed grass (*Calamagrostis × acutiflora* 'Overdam').

In the foreground are radiant martagon lilies (*Lilium martagon* 'Orange Marmalade') and Japanese tree lilac (*Syringa reticulata*) in front of a large clump of shuttlecock ferns (*Matteuccia struthiopteris*) planted more than seventy years ago. The grass in the pond is bottle sedge (*Carex rostrata*), and Regel's threewingnut grows beneath the eaves of the house. A clipped hedge of alpine currant (*Ribes alpinum* 'Schmidt') gives structure to the small garden, with bugbane (*Actaea simplex* 'Brunette') behind it.

OPPOSITE In early summer late-flowering tulips, such as the wine-red *Tulipa* 'Merlot' interspersed with 'White Triumphator' and brownish-black 'Havran', are still flowering among perennials, including the white bleeding heart (*Dicentra formosa* 'Aurora') and salmon-pink foxgloves (*Digitalis purpurea* 'Apricot'), here grown as an annual.

LEFT The same bed in early August showcases masterwort (*Astrantia major* 'Superstar' syn. 'White Giant') and Menzies' burnet (*Sanguisorba menziesii*), a long-lasting combination for this partially shaded position.

expanding into the natural areas around it. These untouched natural surroundings will remain untouched for as long as we are here. At the same time, we wanted to invite the much-loved river landscape into the garden by highlighting new views and perspectives.

The entrance to the garden

We kept the entrance relatively open and spacious to make it easier to clear snow. On one side the natural vegetation has been preserved, and on the other is a red barn from a bygone age. This is a piece of cultural history that we surrounded with beds of shrubs and perennials, edged by granite blocks, some of which are taken from the foundations of an old house nearby.

As protection against winds from the north we erected a black-painted fence, and in the best south-facing position against it we planted our beloved Manchurian walnut (*Juglans mandshurica* cv. Hammarö), which needed to be moved to have more space. The tree was brought back as a seedling from an expedition to Asia conducted by the Swedish University of Agriculture in the 1980s. Planted thirty years ago, it was still no more than 6 metres tall when we reworked the garden, and was happy to be moved. A Regel's threewingnut (*Tripterygium regelii* 'Tiara') comes from the same collection. It was planted at the same time and now covers large parts of the entrance facade. But what gives the entrance most of its character is the view of

By the middle of the year, the early summer flowering is at its peak: closest to the house is catmint (*Nepeta* x *faassenii* 'Walker's Low'), in front of a combination of late-flowering white perennials. In the foreground, beneath the old apple tree, are white masterwort and bugbane – all valuable secondary planting, with catmint a clear favourite. To the left of the path is a carpet of hazelwort (*Asarum europaeum*), which in the spring is filled with white fritillaries. To the right a dense border of goatsbeard (*Aruncus aethusifolius*) encloses a bed of Himalayan blue poppies (*Meconopsis baileyi* syn. *betonicifolia*) and white martagon lilies (*Lilium martagon* 'Album').

SUMMER PERENNIALS

By early June the fern-leaf peonies (*Paeonia tenuifolia*) and Veitch's peonies (*P. veitchii*) are in flower, but summer really arrives only when the meadows in the surrounding landscape are in bloom for midsummer. By then the following are all flowering in our garden: catmint – Norrland's lavender – violets, blue phlox, granny's bonnet, daylilies, goatsbeard and various forms of masterwort.

SPRING PERENNIALS

There is nothing sweeter than when the first pulmonaria emerges and is discovered by an overwintering bumblebee as soon as the snow retreats. Oxlips (*Primula elatior*) and simple pale blue wood anemones (*Anemone nemorosa* 'Robinsoniana') follow, and even if the bloodroot (*Sanguinaria canadensis*) that has been here since my mother's time can't quite keep up, I still tend it lovingly for the short period of flower that it gives. Spring is crowned by trilliums, foremost among them the magnificent great white trillium (*Trillium grandiflorum*). As in most gardens, pale blue forget-me-nots seed themselves happily into any available spot.

BULBS

Blue carpets of Siberian squill (*Scilla sibirica*) are as reliable as they are delightful, even at this latitude, as are spring crocuses (*Crocus vernus*) and blue glory-of-the-snow (*S. forbesii* syn. *Chionodoxa forbesii*). Snake's-head fritillaries (*Fritillaria meleagris*) also cope well, and the white form looks particularly good in carpets of hazelwort (*Asarum europaeum*).

Other bulbs that spread include all varieties of martagon lily. My favourites are the white form and the whisky-coloured 'Orange Marmalade', both powerful lilies that give character to beds of green foliage.

By contrast, tulips and daffodils are not as reliable. We plant new ones each autumn, even if there are exceptions; *Tulipa turkestanica*, *Narcissus poeticus* 'Actaea' and *N.* 'Thalia' come back year after year.

SUMMER FLOWERS

1. White martagon lily (*Lilium martagon* 'Album')
2. Violas (*Viola × williamsii* 'Belmont Blue')
3. Veitch's peonies (*Paeonia veitchii*)
4. Narcissus (*Narcissus poeticus* 'Actaea')
5. Gentian speedwell (*Veronica gentianoides*)
6. Mountain deathcamas (*Zigadenus elegans* syn. *Anticlea elegans*)
7. Fair maids of France (*Ranunculus aconitifolius* 'Flore Pleno')
8. Shuttlecock fern (*Matteuccia struthiopteris*)
9. Lilac (*Syringa vulgaris* 'Norrfjärden')

- A House
- B Pavilion
- C Orangery
- D Greenhouse
- E Entrance
- F Garden
- G Kitchen garden
- H Nature

1

2

3

4

5

6

7

8

9

a large hazel tree from the 1970s, underplanted with spring-flowering ground cover. Double wood anemones make a carpet with primroses, scilla, pulmonaria and red epimediums, which, together with large shuttlecock ferns, form beautiful swathes of foliage in the summer. This delightful composition, which has developed over sixty years, lends the rebuilt garden a quality that would have been impossible from scratch, given that it is the result of the passage of time.

The Queen's Lunch

We felt a great longing for a spacious outdoor room, positioned as a hub on the boundary between nature and the garden. Taking inspiration from my *Daily Telegraph* garden at the Chelsea Flower Show in 2009, the pavilion was constructed with a gently inclined roof on a frame of glulam (glue-laminated wood) and steel beams, with walls and roof of toughened glass. At one end there was space for a small woodshed with timber walls, which also gave

OPPOSITE The path of granite slabs leads to the barn, which dates from the 1850s and stands in front of a granite disc that evokes a millstone. In the foreground are bronze serviceberry and mountain deathcamas in a carpet of hazelwort.

BELOW The pavilion is furnished with containers that have hidden wheels, and in them white standard roses and oleander trees are underplanted with dark-leaved heuchera, white mandevilla and large-leaved maidenhair ferns. In the foreground grow heliotrope and white lobelia.

RIGHT Many of the oldest plants in the garden are grouped around the steps down to the river, such as the double pink scented *Paeonia lactiflora* 'Sarah Bernhardt', with double white *Achillea ptarmica* var. *multiplex* 'Boule de Neige' and old-fashioned auriculas close to the steps. The dark-leaved heuchera and various salvias are more recent additions. Details of the beds on the right can be seen on pages 26–7.

OVERLEAF Pale blue *Amsonia* 'Blue Ice', pink Byzantine gladioli (*Gladiolus communis* subsp. *byzantinus*) and white fleabane (*Erigeron* 'Sommerneuschnee') are tried-and-tested plants in the garden, while *Salvia* × *sylvestris* 'Schneehügel' and the pale violet-blue *S. nemorosa* 'Salute Ice Blue' are more recent acquaintances.

PAGE 27 The best-loved and longest-cultivated favourites in the garden are the Himalayan blue poppy and white martagon lily.

solidity to the entire structure. The floor, which was laid with metre-square granite slabs, has its own history: it comes from that show garden. Since Queen Elizabeth II visited that garden, there was room for a little humour, and we named the pavilion 'The Queen's Lunch'. Even after ten years, the elegant glass roof still works, regardless of heavy snow or bright summer sun.

The pavilion is next to a small nineteenth-century shed, painted black, and this offers an interesting encounter between modernism and tradition. The pavilion's black frame of glulam and steel and the transparency of the glass blur the line between past and present. Long mornings are spent here, and almost all meals eaten, from early spring, when snow is still on the ground, to autumn with its flaming colours. The pavilion has become our 'bird's nest' in the middle of nature.

In a similar way, we reused a pond from Chelsea. We thought it would be a new paradise for frogs, but they didn't agree. Still, the rippling, trickling water adds a dimension that we appreciate – with or without frogs.

The garden takes shape

In front of the house, in a prime south-facing position, we made narrow parallel walkways with intersecting lines that frame the grass and planting areas. The paths were laid out in such a way that valuable older plants could be saved, among them a few apple trees, snowball bushes and some gnarled hawthorn trees. The paths also reinforce the sight lines down to the rapids and through to the surrounding countryside.

The garden slopes down towards the river by means of steps and walls of solid granite, partly for increased accessibility, and partly to make the most of the microclimate on the south-facing slope. This sunny space has always been central to the garden, and it is home to plants that need more warmth. The granite is an asset in itself because it stores heat on sunny

Red masterwort (*Astrantia major* 'Hadspen Blood') and pale speedwell (*Veronicastrum virginicum* 'Album') are interspersed with older forms of speedwell and spurge. Species grown as annuals, such as *Ammi majus* 'Graceland', sweet scabious (*Scabiosa atropurpurea*) and white-flowered rose campion (*Lychnis coronaria* 'Alba'), give the planting a feeling of a summer meadow.

The rapids below the garden form part of a Natura 2000 (EU protected) area, and are thereby safeguarded for the future. This is a remarkable environment that changes dramatically with the seasons.

ABOVE The strawberry bed in front of the orangery is backed by citrus trees that spend the summer outside in the best south-facing position.

OPPOSITE Our little kitchen garden with a touch of the cottage garden is in a prime south-facing position and contains summer vegetables and flowers for cutting. Sweet peas grow up the netting to engulf us in fragrance late in the summer. In the background are the tall pines and firs of the surroundings. Behind the greenhouse is the willow (*Salix caprea*), the most valuable tree in the spring with its early supply of nectar and pollen.

days, making it wonderful for bare feet in the summer, as well as for plants that love warmth.

To link the new plantings to the outer edges of the garden, I used dense, low-growing perennials, which also help to prevent weeds from growing. For border plantings in full sun, I used lavender-blue catmint (*Nepeta × faassenii* 'Walker's Low' and 'Cat's Meow'), similarly hued violas (*Viola × williamsii* 'Belmont Blue'), white horned pansy (*V. cornuta* 'Alba') and ice-blue speedwell (*Veronica gentianoides*). For edging in partial shade, lady's mantle (*Alchemilla mollis*), goatsbeard (*Aruncus aethusifolius*), red barrenwort (*Epimedium × rubrum*), hazelwort (*Asarum europaeum*) and white Siberian bugloss (*Brunnera macrophylla* 'Betty Bowring') work very well, even if the last of these requires care to get it through the winter.

Kitchen garden deluxe

When we had the opportunity to take over an area of land outside the garden in a lovely, south-facing position, we realized that it was the ultimate location for a longed-for kitchen garden. There was also space for a greenhouse, vegetable plot and orangery.

Vegetable garden

In larch-framed raised beds that form an area totalling 13 square metres, we grow most of the vegetables we need: all sorts of lettuce, radishes, spinach, rocket, dill, carrots, beetroot, French beans and peas. Provided they're sown around 20 May, under horticultural fleece that is removed a month later, the summer light makes it possible to start harvesting the first crops after just five weeks. We grow strawberries and currants in open ground, where there is also room for summer flowers – and my absolute favourites: English varieties of sweet pea. Growing a little of many varieties, and sowing at intervals, is the best way to ensure that there is always something to harvest throughout the short summer.

Greenhouse

The first of the lettuce, dill and rocket is grown in raised beds inside the cedar-wood greenhouse, followed by tomatoes and cucumbers. We also use the greenhouse to raise many plants that are later used in the garden, among them summer flowers and lilies that we plant out in pots.

The orangery: a Mediterranean dream

After creating and furnishing many public glazed rooms and orangeries in private gardens, it was finally time to plan one of my own. Built of spruce, with glass on three sides and a solid wall on the fourth (north) side, this has become our great love in recent years and – as always when it comes to glazed structures – is now one size too small for all the ideas and needs that have arisen as time has gone by.

Citrus trees, jasmine, bougainvillea and mimosa overwinter in the orangery, as do resting tree ferns, orchids and brugmansia. In the summer, when most of the plants have moved out, the orangery provides space for parties and social gatherings. It is perhaps the ultimate luxury, for us, to be surrounded by Mediterranean plants even as we gaze out in darkness across a frozen landscape beneath the northern lights.

Technology

The winter temperature in the orangery is about 12–15°C, which is good for dormant Mediterranean plants, and we can quickly raise it to 20°C by lighting a fire in the open hearth. Industrial triple-glazed windows, well-insulated wooden walls, and stone floors with heating pipes provide an even indoor climate that isn't affected by the changing weather outside – a necessity in the type of winter that prevails so far north.

We use wireless technology to control the underfloor heating, ventilation and blinds. This is an uncomplicated and energy-efficient way of maintaining a stable indoor climate. When the sun comes out in February, the afternoons can

LATE SUMMER AND AUTUMN PERENNIALS

Favourites that give the beds volume in August include bugbane, white speedwell and the lavender-blue form (*Veronicastrum virginicum* 'Lavendelturm'), violet rue (*Thalictrum* 'Elin'), blue and white forms of Chinese meadow rue (*T. delavayi* 'Splendide' and 'Splendide White'), Menzies' burnet (*Sanguisorba menziesii*), white-flowered slender-leaved burnet (*S. tenuifolia* var. 'Alba') and lavender-blue sea holly (*Eryngium planum*). Of the phloxes, the white autumn phlox (*Phlox paniculata* 'David') and the pale pink *P. paniculata* 'Rosa Pastell' are favourites.

become warm, and the temperature is regulated by ventilation openings that are controlled automatically by sensors. Blinds on the outer facade – also controlled by a sensor – keep the sun's heat out. In the summer the double doors are always open, providing the room with a gentle and much-needed breeze.

During the summer, unwelcome insects are kept away with the help of mosquito nets. In the early spring we use natural predators if we have problems with pests as the plants come to life. For instance, we use predatory mites against spider mites, and ladybirds against the mealybugs that always appear on the citrus plants in the spring sunshine.

Shrubs and trees

All the larger bushes and shrubby trees we added to the garden are in the Swedish E-mark system for plants, which ensures, among other things, their hardiness (see page 228). We chose a few varieties to recur throughout the beds, to tie the different parts of the garden together.

Spring in nature begins here with the flowering of willow (*Salix caprea*) followed by bird cherry (*Prunus padus*). In our garden the hazel (*Corylus avellana* cv. Torslunda) flowers at the same time, with greenish-yellow pendants that sparkle like crystal chandeliers in the bright light. Our garden is in the northernmost distribution area for hazel, and the flowers may be simple, but they make a difference. This is followed by the serviceberry (*Amelanchier laevis* cv. Bäcklösa), which produces large clusters of white flowers in late May, set against striking coppery foliage. After this come the Sargent crab apple (*Malus toringo* var. *sargentii* 'Eskilstuna') and Siberian crab apple (*M. baccata*), their blossom contrasting with the coppery stems of the Manchurian cherry (*Prunus maackii*).

In early June the garden is enveloped by the scent that rises from the large, fragrant lavender-blue flowers of lilac (*Syringa vulgaris* 'Norrfjärden'[PBR]). The Japanese tree lilac (*S. reticulata* cv. Enskede) follows, with its large, creamy-white, lightly scented clusters of flowers, which, together with the globe-shaped blooms of the snowball bush (*Viburnum opulus* 'Strömsund'), carry us into the summer.

Protection from the elements

To protect our plantings from northerly winds, we use buildings and fences to optimal effect, but you can also create a microclimate by planting solitary tall bushes and smaller trees. This creates the feeling of the edge of a forest or woodland, and offers the sort of creeping shade that many garden plants thrive in.

A thin layer of leaves on top of the soil is extremely valuable for overwintering perennials with their buds above ground. A layer of snow on frozen ground is better than on unfrozen ground, which benefits fungi and pests. A mild winter climate at this latitude is also harmful because the roots of perennials can easily be destroyed by severe night frosts. I place a thin layer of dry leaves over frozen ground, and this protects the plants when the spring sun appears.

Giving plants a plentiful supply of organic matter during the growing season is invaluable for good development and overwintering. Natural soil is always the best starting point, although manufactured composts have become increasingly common. The best of these have been developed to contain both compost and biochar (a type of charcoal), which is a big step forwards. The addition of manure and compost is always preferable to cheap, fertilized peat, which is unsustainable and gives only short-term results because it decomposes so quickly.

My experience is that perennials grow best if they are planted in the spring, preferably in a bed that was prepared the previous autumn, so that the soil has had time to settle. The soil level can be adjusted and the surface smoothed out before planting.

At the end of March winter lets go of the landscape. Temperatures above freezing mean that the snow melts and the migratory birds of spring – swans, geese and grebes – land on the first open stretch of water. Spring is at the door. It is a time full of buds and promise, and my favourite of the year.

City Hall Park

A city park in the far north

The reconstruction of an urban park in Sweden's most northerly university city, with new expectations and requirements, but also with respect for the history and climate of the site. This was how I interpreted the task when I was asked in 2013 to renew Umeå's venerable city park.

A large part of our history is to be found in our urban spaces. Swedish cities began to develop rapidly in the second half of the nineteenth century, and our city parks were laid out during that period of expansion. One important source of inspiration was the English landscaped park, which formed the model for many of the parks that were established at that time.

The English style was introduced to Sweden by Fredrik Magnus Piper, when in 1781 he presented a proposal for Haga Park in Stockholm. One characteristic of this style was a gentle delineation of paths and beds, with long sight lines and beautiful views across the landscape. The ambition was to design beds in which the plants would be able to develop their natural beauty, ideally with contrasts in form and colour, and with changes of light and shade. This was the ideal of the English landscaped park.

The modern history of the town of Umeå begins when the wooden city on the Ume River burned down in June 1888. (By a quirk of fate, the town of Sundsvall, 250 kilometres to the south, was also ravaged by fire on the same warm, dry summer's day.) At the time, Umeå was a small port of 3,000 inhabitants, and was relatively affluent. There were small boatyards and sawmills that made their owners wealthy from the resources provided by the large forests inland. After the fire, Umeå was rebuilt along neoclassical lines, with paved streets arranged in a grid and lined with birch trees. The wide streets were designed to function as firebreaks. As a result, the birches became the symbol of the town, and today Umeå is known as the City of Birches.

The city was reconstructed with the characteristic wooden buildings that still stand today. A few imposing structures were made of brick and stone, such as the customs house, the main church, banks and the city hall, and most of these were built along the central axis that runs from the railway station down to the river.

City Hall Park was laid out in 1896 on the slope in front of City Hall, in the English style, with winding gravel paths and symmetrical raised beds for annuals. These were known as 'wallpaper beds', and something similar was then in fashion throughout Europe. More avenues of birches were planted to frame the park, and the central axis was emphasized using lines of maples.

As Swedish towns expanded and became more populous, so knowledge and experience in the horticultural sector grew. Towards the end of the nineteenth century most towns acquired municipal parks, as well as smaller, well-maintained parks close to their railway stations. The layout of these parks differed between the north and south of the country, according to financial resources and local conditions, such as climate and topography.

Such parks originally contained local plants, and in Umeå many of the trees were birches and rowans, combined with other simple garden plants, such as hawthorn and lilac. But it was

Magnificent newly planted limes (*Tilia cordata*) frame the surroundings of City Hall.

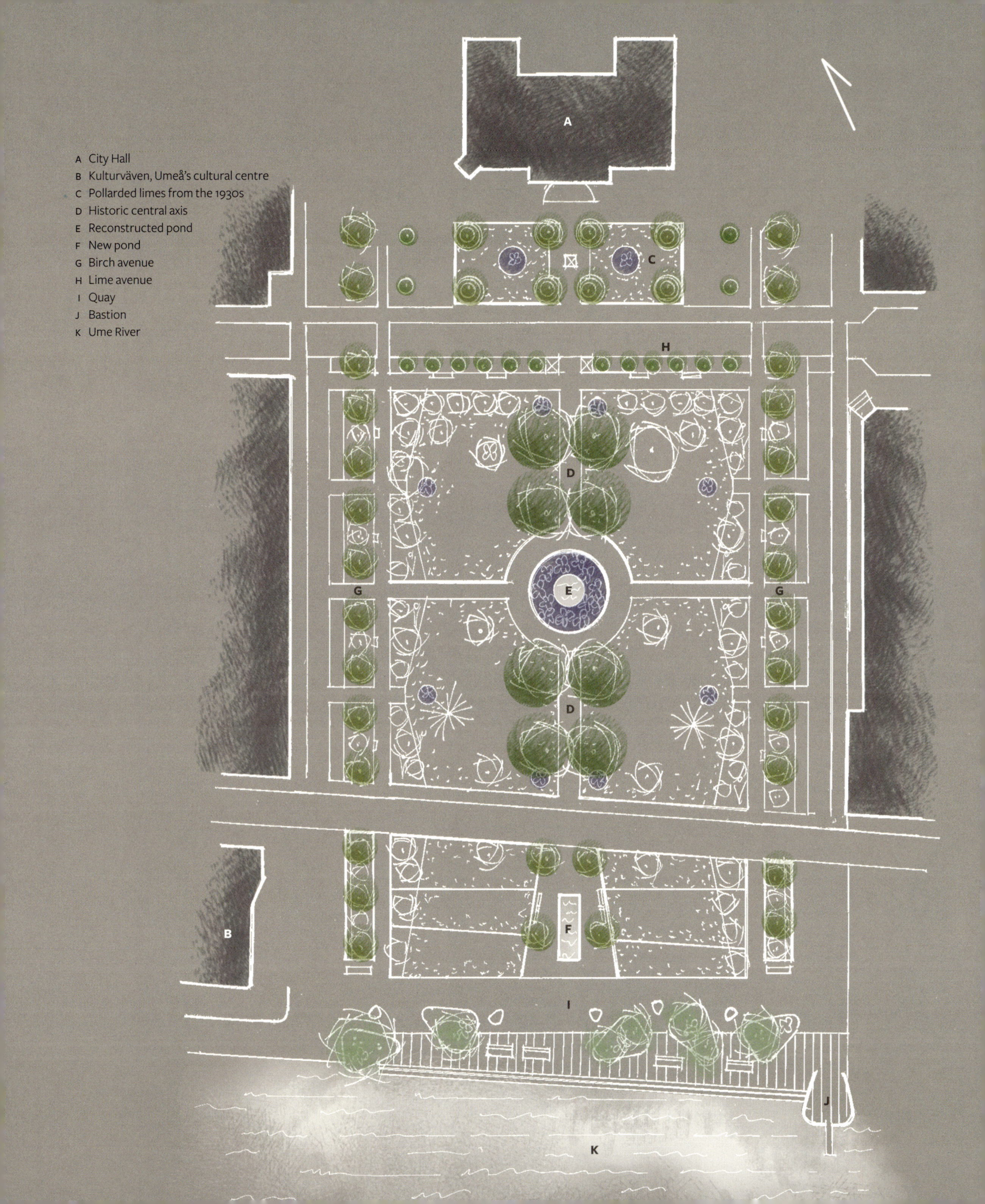
A City Hall
B Kulturväven, Umeå's cultural centre
C Pollarded limes from the 1930s
D Historic central axis
E Reconstructed pond
F New pond
G Birch avenue
H Lime avenue
I Quay
J Bastion
K Ume River

the hand-picked summer plants in the beds that gave City Hall Park its floral splendour, and this remains the case to the present day.

Umeå is today a growing university city with about 30,000 students. They have contributed to both a thriving cultural life and the development of the park from a classic place to stroll to the most popular outdoor space in the city. Part of the park's appeal lies in the changing of the seasons, not least during dark winter evenings when the northern lights form a dramatic play of light above the city.

In advance of Umeå's year as European Capital of Culture in 2014, it was decided to take a collective approach to this public space, which created a unique opportunity to refine the entire cityscape. Even if the park reflected its origins, there was an opportunity to reconstruct the historic basic plan with modern additions. Valuable plant material could be preserved – the large apple trees, for instance – but at the same time my intention was to refine the park so that it reflects contemporary life.

In Umeå, where nature is never far away, the park has an important role as a public meeting place. City Hall and the other stone buildings that surround the park foster a sense of security and warmth, which is reinforced by the south-facing slope down towards the wide, rugged river. The surrounding buildings provided good conditions for an upgrade of the city's 'living room'.

Sometimes coincidence can make all the difference. On a visit to one of Europe's largest nurseries, in northern Germany, where I was actually looking for plants for Chelsea 2013, I saw something that piqued my interest. One of the fields where trees were grown contained cone-shaped lime trees with huge root balls, dug up to be replanted and eventually become even bigger park trees – a German speciality. All twenty of them were moved to Umeå a few years later to frame City Hall from the south,

Perennials, such as masterwort, salvia and speedwell, with summer annuals, including verbenas, create the conditions for biodiversity in the middle of the city.

and to connect the park to its immediate surroundings. In front of City Hall there were already 800-year-old pollarded Kaiser limes (*Tilia × europaea* 'Pallida') surrounding a statue of the founder of the city, Gustav II Adolf. With the new trees, these frame the urban space in a clear, dignified way.

The original elements of the park – the central fountain and the old trees – were important prerequisites for the redesign. The basic idea was to enhance the symmetry and add new entrances, as well as large strips of open grass along the sides. To make the sloping park more accessible, low walls of granite for sitting on were placed along the paths, an approach that also took care of the differences in level.

Along the main axis from City Hall down to the quay, the old central pond was reconstructed and a new one added on the quayside, with water flowing over the sides. The two ponds form a clear link between City Hall and the river.

The water flows over the sides of the pond, inviting visitors to play.

The entire quayside was given a freer design in dialogue with the architecture and materials of the new cultural centre, Kulturväven (literally 'cultural fabric'). This building, by the Oslo architectural practice Snøhetta, is a meeting place for cultural activities of all kinds. Its transparent and white glazed sections bring to mind the striations of birch trunks and breaking ice, and this became the theme of the quayside. The irregular black-and-white pattern of the birches was reinterpreted in new paving along the quay, with granite slabs in varying sizes and tones. The ice floes of winter lend their shapes to large raised beds framed by granite walls. Some of these hang over the edge of the quay as a reminder of the transience of the ice. The quay ends with a large wooden deck furnished with specially designed glulam recliners and benches of black-painted Norrland spruce. In this way, the scale and structure of Kulturväven were matched by the landscape design.

One spectacular vantage point in the form of a bastion with a large trampoline that extends over the edge of the quay gives a tingling sensation when visitors step out above the rushing water of the river. From there you also get an unforgettable view of the city. This vantage point has become both a meeting place and a contemporary statement.

In the upper part of the park, with its historic central axis lined with maples, the planting areas were reinterpreted in new, sunlit positions, while large beds of perennials and shrubs were created along the side paths to both frame and make room for attractive open areas of grass.

The illumination, by the lighting architect Torbjörn Eliasson, is carefully balanced to enhance the entire urban space, particularly the central axis with its ponds, and the open area on the quayside.

The quayside has been clad with large, dark-pigmented blocks of glulam.

The section of the park by the river has quickly come to be appreciated by everyone. With its large, open area and reclining seats it has become an enticing meeting place and a destination in the winter as much as in the summer. Even at the darkest time of year, the lighting – and sometimes also the northern lights – makes it beautiful.

Trees and shrubs

Avenues of birch trees are a must in Umeå. In the far north, birches turn green with new leaves in the middle of May, and with the graphic texture of their bark they form beautiful frames for the streets. Replanting the avenues along the long sides of the park with white-stemmed silver birches (*Betula pendula* 'Splendor White') was part of the plan from the outset.

It was also obvious to me that the central axis of maples should be extended all the way down to the quay. I planted large horse chestnuts to give the park a solid bulk of trees in the future. More exotic inclusions, such as the Manchurian walnut (*Juglans mandshurica* cv. Hammarö), will develop less because of the northerly location. Ulleung Island rowans (*Sorbus ulleungensis* 'Dodong'), on the other hand, in both tree and bush form will provide airy crowns and strong autumn colour after just a few years.

After the reconstruction, old crab apples were replanted on the quayside, complemented by large specimens of the variety 'Evereste' in bush form.

Along the sides of the park, large areas of the prostrate, spreading conifer Siberian carpet cypress (*Microbiota decussata*) are interspersed with symmetrically planted solitary shrubs chosen for their flowers or autumn colour. Spring blossom is provided by serviceberries (*Amelanchier laevis* cv. Bäcklösa), Ulleung Island rowans and crab apples (*Malus toringo* var. *sargentii* 'Eskilstuna'), while white-flowered panicle hydrangeas (*Hydrangea paniculata* 'Great Star') provide plentiful autumn flowers. Several katsura trees (*Cercidiphyllum japonicum*) were planted for their beautiful framework of branches and their buds, as well as their autumn colour and gingerbread scent. Maples and Ulleung Island rowans give the park its fiery autumn colour thanks to the difference between the cool nights and high daytime temperatures.

Perennials

In recent years perennial plants have made their entrance into urban parks, a much-needed addition to annual summer bedding. The planting areas on the south-facing slopes of City Hall Park provide favourable conditions with good drainage, and this is valuable not least because icy winters dramatically reduce the survival rate of perennials, when frozen water can be left standing around the plants.

My aim was to use perennials to create airy beds with the feel of a summer meadow. The colours are blue, pink and white, with touches of silver-grey. By choosing plants with a long flowering period, we can stretch this experience to cover the whole season. The concept is based on a limited number of different perennials planted in varying combinations to create harmony and variety, as well as favourable conditions for biodiversity in the centre of the city.

The strict symmetry of the new layout could be compared to that of a Baroque garden. The classic box edgings that are so strongly associated with that period are reinterpreted through the use of the beautiful blue-grey moor grass (*Sesleria nitida*) to frame the planting beds.

The blue flowers of the narrow-leaved lungwort (*Pulmonaria* 'Blue Ensign') and bulbs give spring colour. Summer interest is provided by perennials of varying heights, such as blue catmint (*Nepeta* × *faassenii* 'Cat's Meow' and 'Walker's Low'), red and white masterwort (*Astrantia major* 'Hadspen Blood' and 'Superstar' syn. 'White Giant'), great burnet (*Sanguisorba officinalis*), pinkish-white speedwell (*Veronicastrum virginicum* 'Album') and violet-blue *Salvia nemorosa* 'Caradonna', while creamy-red autumn phlox (*Phlox paniculata* 'Rosa Pastell') and violet-blue giant hyssop (*Agastache* 'Black Adder') provide late summer flowers in the upper part of the park. In the corresponding beds on the quayside, the phlox and hyssop are replaced with gentian (*Gentiana makinoi*), which, with its intense blue colouring, prolongs the flowering season all the way into October.

Bulbs

For early perennial bulbs, I chose striped squill (*Puschkinia scilloides*) and Siberian squill (*Scilla sibirica*). To emphasize the early shoots of the perennials I used late-flowering tulips, such as the soft rose-coloured 'Pink Diamond' and brownish-black 'Queen of Night', as well as lily-flowered cultivars, the brown-red 'Havran', purple-red 'Merlot' and 'White Triumphator'. Other bulbs include dark *Camassia leichtlinii* subsp. *suksdorfii* 'Caerulea' and an old-fashioned narcissus, 'Actaea'. They are planted in the perennial beds to enhance the summer display,

A shimmering oval bench of black terrazzo.

while martagon lilies (*Lilium martagon* 'Orange Marmalade') lend a warm copper colour to the beds at the height of the summer.

The islands on the quayside

The large triangular beds on the quay are planted with fields of vigorous perennials and grasses in simple combinations. All include patches of feather reed grass (*Calamagrostis × acutiflora* 'Overdam') that are separated from areas of perennials, among them pink great burnet (*Sanguisorba officinalis* 'Pink Tanna'), the blue clump-forming *Iris* 'Silver Edge', pink-red masterwort (*Astrantia major* 'Roma'), the early yellow daylily (*Hemerocallis lilioasphodelus*) and the late pale yellow daylily (*H. citrina*).

Many of the grass plantings on the quayside include great burnet, which gives character in the late summer. The powerful yet simple and strict planting on the quay differs from the

LEFT Pinkish-white spires of speedwell and red masterwort are seen in front of newly planted maples (*Acer platanoides*), with white-stemmed silver birches (*Betula pendula* 'Splendor White') in the background. All are valuable for biodiversity in this urban location. The backdrop is a tall hedge of white *Thuja occidentalis* 'Brabant'.

ABOVE The wooden decking is furnished with specially designed reclining benches in the same material. The granite-framed islands are filled with feather reed grass and perennials.

Clouds above the snow on the Ume River in March.

OPPOSITE The large transplanted crab apples stand out against the black-and-white glazed facade of Kulturväven, while the reclining benches wait for the snow to recede.

more romantic planting in the upper part of the park, a deliberate way of creating character and variation.

Summer flowers

In northern Swedish cities, as in many worldwide, the use of bedding plants in public settings has a longer tradition than the use of perennials. This dates back to the late nineteenth century, when public parks were established. At this time many had their own greenhouses and cold frames, for the labour-intensive process of propagating scores of summer plants by seeds and cuttings. Plants were hardened off in the cold frames before being bedded out in mid-June, at which time it would be certain that the last nocturnal frosts of early summer were over.

Umeå is one of the few towns and cities in Sweden that has been able to maintain plant production in its own greenhouses for an entire century. Today large quantities of bedding plants are still produced: annuals and more, but also exotic plants that are overwintered from year to year. A great deal of knowledge has been accumulated over the years, and it is certainly needed if the bare beds are to be filled each year with summer-flowering plants. Every year new schemes are planned, to provide something new and create interest in the city's flowerbeds.

All the beds for summer flowers in City Hall Park are filled according to the same principle, except for the planting area by the central pond. There, the same fuchsias that have been associated with this area since the early 1960s are replanted. These are the variety 'Beacon', with stiff, gently curved branches and teardrop-shaped purple and red flowers. Because of their age, these fuchsias have great symbolic value, and are planted in a carpet of low-growing summer flowers. The intention with this planting around the circular pond is to create a historical connection to a bygone era.

Stadsbibliotek

Rydboholm Castle

A Baroque garden for our time

A desire to revive the Baroque garden at Rydboholm Castle led to a collaboration over many years. The plan was to combine the formal Baroque style and the seasons of Swedish nature, with all the biodiversity they offer.

It is a sunny day in early summer the first time I meet Countess Elisabeth Douglas at Rydboholm Castle. We sit on a bench in front of a very old avenue of limes. It is known as the Avenue of Sighs because over time the treetops have grown together to shut out the sky, leaving everything beneath them in gloom. In the light in front of us lie green lawns sprinkled with spring flowers, alliums and majestic crown imperials. They glow as if from a bygone age, and remind Elisabeth fondly of her childhood. Together we gaze out at the remaining traces of that childhood, hidden among the greenery. This is the story of the refinement of a culturally historic park into a piece of Swedish contemporary cultural heritage.

Rydboholm in the past

Rydboholm began as a late medieval farm in Uppland that belonged to the Sture and Vasa families before becoming the estate of the Brahe family for almost 400 years. Most of the walls of the present castle were once part of the building constructed by Per Brahe the Elder in about 1550.

The earliest known illustration of the site is a copperplate engraving dating from 1660, when the castle appeared in the comprehensive publication *Suecia Antiqua et Hodierna* (Ancient and Modern Sweden). It shows a grand fortified manor house with high defensive walls. The castle is also well documented in Karin Andersson's book *Rydboholm: Från befäst sätesgård till empireslott* (From Fortified Manor to Empire-era Castle; 2002).

The engraving includes a sketchy outline of the garden with strictly delineated blocks. At the end of one path, a tall gate can be seen in a wall that separates the garden from the natural landscape beyond, but which was probably never built.

The Baroque garden as stylistic ideal was developed in the seventeenth century by the French landscape artist André Le Nôtre, whose most famous work – at the Château de Vaux-le-Vicomte outside Paris – is very well preserved.

At Rydboholm the style is characterized by strict avenues, which give way at the periphery of the park to free-growing trees. There is documentation of some of the details of the Baroque garden, such as the brickwork, steps and sculptures, but no designer has ever been identified, although there is mention of contact with the Swedish court gardener Christian Horleman at the time the garden was created.

During the 1660s and 70s Nils Brahe transformed Rydboholm into a Baroque garden in line with the taste of the times. There are no descriptions of the floral splendour he introduced, but there are records of the purchase of box plants, ornamental trees, fruit trees and currant bushes, as well as cloches, forcing beds for the cultivation of melons, and classical cast-iron urns.

After extensive blasting of rocks and levelling of the ground around the castle, the garden was laid out in a scheme of regular grass parterres surrounded by avenues of trees, with a central axis running north to south. In front of the south side of the castle was a parterre with steps and terraces that concluded in an arc facing the water of Kyrkviken. This was the site of *Mercury* by Adriaen de Vries, one of the foremost sculptors of the time. Grass parterres were also laid out to the north of the castle, here with a building, probably a gazebo, terminating the central axis as a focal point. As a result of the building-up of the site, the remains of the moat were eventually transformed into two mirrored ponds. The western one had a rounded end, while that on the north side of the castle was laid out as a rectangular carp pond.

The history of the park

In the early eighteenth century the Baroque park took on its final shape. A large fruit and

A copperplate engraving from *Suecia Antiqua et Hodierna* (1660) showing the castle with its defensive walls on the shores of Kyrkviken.

Tall beech hedges and clipped cones of cedar were planted to create fully fledged garden rooms – a way to cut the growth time by several generations. In the foreground are crown imperials in a bed of narcissi edged with hybrid yew.

vegetable garden was established to the east of the castle, from which the surplus was sold locally. An orangery facilitated the cultivation of citrus, agave, standard box trees, oleander, myrtle, figs, mulberries, pomegranates and laurel trees, as well as fragrant jasmine.

At the end of the eighteenth century Rydboholm was in the hands of Magnus Fredrik Brahe, a nobleman who was well educated by the standards of the time and close to the royal court. A drawing from 1801 shows his transformation of the park. The avenues and ponds remain, but the addition of the English park to the west of the Baroque garden will forever be associated with him. In line with the fashion of the time, the park gained many romantic adornments, such as temples and memorial stones.

It wasn't until about 1900 that the castle was modernized and its agriculture rationalized, and the maintenance of the English-style park began to approach traditional forestry. Today, thanks to the care of the current owners, it has been restored, and retains much of its original

A floral embroidery of wild flowers set in sand contains cowslips, pasque flowers and red species tulips – a smorgasbord for insects in the spring.

character in terms of roads, vegetation and structures. Each redesign of the castle park reflects the early development of garden design in Sweden. Since the turn of the last century the English park has been a popular destination for visitors, but the Baroque garden was closed in the 1970s.

The impact of history is very clear at Rydboholm, not least in the tradition of planting oak trees. The Gustav Vasa oak was planted in the sixteenth century, and King Karl XIV Johan planted some stately oaks behind the castle in 1834. Sadly, the Gustav Vasa oak fell in a storm in 2018, but it has been preserved on the site.

Renovating the park

A large project of this kind requires artistic competence on many levels, and the entire plan must be anchored in the soul of the place, the *genius loci*. For me, the significant raising of the land over the past 500 years and the regular avenues of limes provided a natural way in. I was struck deeply by the castle's location on the shores of Kyrkviken, with a view of untouched nature yet at the same time close to the centre of Stockholm.

Reconstructions of green cultural heritage are valued for their own sake in most of Europe, while we in Sweden value what has been added over time. A process of free renewal is affirmed when the traces of history run dry. Working on Rydboholm allowed the space to value the heritage while adding upgrades that reflect our own time. The existing structure of avenues was a defining feature of the project. We also decided early in the process that detailed, high-level technical facilities should form the basis of future care and maintenance, combining traditional methods with modern technology.

The lake parterre

The stone walls in front of the castle, known as the lake parterre, had been ruined by the roots of the old lime trees as they grew, and by trees falling in autumn storms. They had to be rebuilt from scratch. This became the first part of the project, in which history formed the basis of the work to create a cohesive environment. We were helped in this by photographs from the early twentieth century.

A local quarry provided granite, which became a wonderful material in the hands of skilled masons. When the walls began to take shape with their steps and forged railings, instead of the power and pomp that Baroque gardens usually express, a feeling of humility became apparent.

Following an illustration from 1801, the grass parterres were given classical swirls of shaped sward, while the storm-felled limes in front of the castle were replaced with

OPPOSITE Dawn over the old carp pond, with the more recent additions of a yew parterre and clipped conifers.

BELOW The stream passes through a number of smaller, planted ponds to capture excess nutrients from the cultivated landscape before the water reaches the moat. Several varieties of narcissus are planted on the banks.

A flowering crab apple – Elisabeth Douglas's favourite tree in the Baroque garden.

symmetrical plantings of fastigiate beech (*Fagus sylvatica*) and copper beech (*F. s.* var. *purpurea*). I also decided to include flowering trees, even though they don't conform to the Baroque ideal. In front of the castle, we planted white-flowered ornamental Japanese cherries (*Prunus* 'Shirotae') and box-edged beds of tall hydrangeas – another element that can be seen in the early twentieth-century photographs.

The statue of Mercury has been replaced with a copy, set in front of the castle in a circular bed of summer flowers. This concept is repeated on a lower terrace with *Copernicus*, a sundial of patinated copper and gold mosaic created in 2020 by the silversmith and jeweller Sebastian Schildt. These two artworks create a bold contrast spanning more than 300 years. In the courtyard are large new containers of blue agapanthus, all of which stem from a single plant that I was once given by Ulla Molin, the mother of modern Swedish garden design.

By slightly exaggerating the scale of the plantings and adornments, a sense of balance is achieved around the castle. A circular granite bench beneath a Kentucky coffee tree (*Gymnocladus dioicus*) in front of the western facade breaks the strict symmetry and gives the place a more understated appearance.

The pictures from the last century show two large cast-iron urns in front of the castle. These were restored and used as the models for new urns, which were placed on the walls we built to create terraces around the castle. The walls were also planted with carpet-forming plants, which give a warm, soft impression. Below the wall closest to the water is a bed of blue and black irises (*Iris* Germanica group 'Superstition' and 'Black Swan') and yellow species tulips (*Tulipa sylvestris*), edged with lavender. Finally, the central axis in front of the castle was enhanced on both sides by clipped globes of evergreen privet in a carpet of spring-flowering blue Balkan anemones (*Anemone blanda*).

The countess's garden

Here, where Elisabeth Douglas once played her childhood games, the remains of wild flowers and overgrown lime avenues were still visible. The site must surely have conjured up dreams of a Baroque garden as early as the seventeenth century. Now, at long last, that could be realized on this fine south-facing slope.

Careful measuring made it possible to design the new park, and it was exciting to rediscover paths with views of the English park. The first thing we did was to reduce the crowns of the overgrown limes dramatically, to extend their life while creating balance and letting in light.

My opinion of the Baroque style is that it can easily become over-formal and boring. That may be why it was soon abandoned outside France and replaced with the more romantic English landscape park. To gain a shared understanding of the classic Baroque style, we went to France, a trip that turned out to be the inspiration for something more playful, something we hadn't originally thought of.

After comprehensive analysis and plenty of discarded sketches, in which I followed the differences in level and the strict idiom of intersecting axes, I finally ended up with sixteen almost equal squares. To make the Baroque more romantic, I chose to incorporate flowering elements to give prominence to nature and biodiversity, as well as reinforcing the changing of the seasons, which isn't something you see in strict Baroque gardens.

With an outer boundary of tall beech hedging and classically shaped beech arches where the paths cross, in the style of the famous French estate Villandry, the garden has a clear frame. This formal structure is complemented by a row of pleached ornamental crab apples (*Malus* 'Evereste'). They provide fantastic white blossom in the spring, as well as autumn colour and winter character, with their masses of tiny red apples.

Intersecting arches of clipped beech, inspired by the French chateau of Villandry, contrast with the pleached flowering crab apples – a conscious break in style. Steel edging removes the labour-intensive work of trimming the edges of the lawns, and gutters made of recycled cobbles emphasize the intricate design.

Along the central axis, two identical long beds were laid out, containing perennials in tones of blue, white and pink. Over the summer these change gradually in character, volume and structure, and a more muted colour palette develops as the autumn approaches.

Four large squares in the centre of the Baroque garden have their own story, relating to the French queen Marie Antoinette. At one of the chateaux we visited in France I was captivated by a cabinet containing part of a dress that had belonged to this notorious eighteenth-century figure. It was of exquisitely embroidered silk with small flowers in luminous pastel colours on a linen base. I couldn't let go of the image, and one day at Rydboholm I realized how the fabric could be transformed into a 600-square-metre embroidery divided into four squares. In a strictly repeating pattern, I planted simple wild flowers, such as cowslips, pasque flowers and white sea thrift, with tomato-red species tulips (*Tulipa eichleri*) on a surface of pale sand. The contrast between the spring-like embroideries and the surrounding formal green texture gives a caramelized feeling of happiness.

This feeling lives on into summer with perennials in tones of white and blue that reflect the sky: among them blue harebells

Early on spring mornings the light falls softly upon the central axis, which in classic Baroque fashion leads the eye towards the wider landscape and Kyrkviken. Beds of perennials enriched by tulips and framed by catmint, with circular granite benches and fountains, and steel supports for climbing plants, give the Baroque garden a contemporary feel. The moat and granite foundations of the castle can be seen in the background. The double avenue of old limes is lovingly cared for, and the castle's surroundings have now gained the richness that the old park lacked.

Clipped hedges of beech and copper beech frame the garden.

(*Campanula rotundifolia*), scented sand pinks (*Dianthus arenarius*), white maiden pinks (*D. deltoides* 'Albiflorus'), silver speedwell (*Veronica spicata* subsp. *incana* 'Silverteppich'), Corsican violets (*Viola corsica*) and small scabious (*Scabiosa columbaria*). To reinforce the contrast between soft and hard, I designed for these embroidery beds formal fountains made from Swedish granite.

Along the beds of perennials that line the central axis, I placed round granite benches to rest on. The axis is edged with gutters made of reused cobbles, which in this sloping garden lead the rainwater away and also provide a decorative pattern amid the strict layout.

The flower-lined promenade along the central axis leads to an orangery in an austere contemporary design by the architect Annette Lindberg. It was there that I first met Elisabeth, and now the place has been enriched with a small garden for potted citrus trees, figs and summer flowers in containers. That garden changes form from year to year, when the annuals are planted. This part of the garden is framed with pleached beech, which forms a 'room' but also lets in much-needed light.

The long sides of the new Baroque garden are completed with low hedges of hybrid yew (*Taxus* × *media* 'Hillii'), which frame beds of scarlet *Geum* 'Totally Tangerine' and silver *Miscanthus sinensis* 'Kleine Fontäne'. In the spring, when the grasses are still small, the garden is lit up by narcissi (*Narcissus poeticus* 'Actaea') and the rust-red crown imperials (*Fritillaria imperialis*) that were once a common sight at the castle. Summer brings more restraint, with whisky-coloured martagon lilies (*Lilium martagon* 'Orange Marmalade') that flower effectively through the growing grass. But the silver grass has its moment of glory in the autumn, with impressive flower spikes that shimmer in the dusk, and this persists throughout the winter until it is time to cut them down in early March.

The exquisite lawns of the parterres are a concession to the ideals of the twentieth century, amply compensated for by the added richness of flowers that encourage biodiversity. The new Baroque garden reaches the gravel paths of the old lime avenue with a range of plants that are native to the site. These half-overgrown gravel paths add a quality that I would probably never have considered if it hadn't already been there.

The parterre on the island

For no discernible reason, the small island to the west of the castle has for many years been called the parterre. It is surrounded by a seventeenth-century moat in the form of a stylized arc, and has now been restored with gently sloping banks and wider mirrors of water. To make the island more accessible, two new bridges were built with classic granite foundations and wooden walkways supported by steel girders. The clay bed of Kyrkviken made construction complicated, but it worked out, and as the bridges took shape, I couldn't help linking the Baroque era with the tulip fever that gripped the Netherlands at the same time. The bridges were therefore given new, hand-forged railings with stylized iron tulips, as a reminder of the grandeur that prevailed when the castle was built.

The central section of the boundary hedge was replaced with copper beech. Clipped pedestals of beech blend into a carpet of periwinkle, and the trunks of the newly planted limes are protected from deer with reed matting.

PREVIOUS PAGES A curved row of Japanese magnolia frames the large beds of perennials in the island parterre and emphasizes the shape of the surrounding moat. In the middle grows a large, solitary serviceberry (*Amelanchier lamarckii*). Upon crossing the bridge, visitors are welcomed by the garden's 'gatekeepers' in the form of clipped beeches. In the foreground are exposed rocks by the castle's woodland area.

BELOW The delicate flower of a star magnolia.

OPPOSITE Camassias grow in drifts beneath a yellow-flowered magnolia with the appropriate name 'Elizabeth'.

The low-lying area around the moat was raised when we received permission from the regional council to replace linden trees that were suffering from severe fungal infections as a result of waterlogging. We chose the variety 'Greenspire' for these new plantings, ensuring a lower avenue in the future, to bring more light to the beds than the previous limes had allowed.

Magnolias

On a visit to a Belgian arboretum the owners of Rydboholm fell in love with flowering magnolias. This inspired a spring symphony in stylized, undulating meadows: a combination of the white hybrid magnolia (*Magnolia* × *loebneri* 'Merrill') with white star magnolia (*M. stellata*) and the pale yellow 'Elizabeth' and 'Yellow Bird'. The magnolias bloom at the same time as the white narcissi 'Actaea' and 'Thalia'. Dark blue *Camassia leichtlinii* subsp. *suksdorfii* 'Caerulea' complete the spring flowering.

On the rounded hillocks, soft Japanese forest grass (*Hakonechloa macra*) forms carpets from which the scented blooms of the regal lily (*Lilium regale*) and rust-red martagon lily (*L. martagon* 'Orange Marmalade') rise during the summer.

The flower garden

Even on the island, I wanted to demonstrate how a flower garden can reflect our times within a historical context. At the entrance we placed so-called gatekeepers of clipped beech, the guards and protectors of the garden, in line with Baroque principles. At the back of the newly planted flower garden I added a large, well-grown serviceberry (*Amelanchier lamarckii*), positioned slightly asymmetrically on a central axis between the bridges. Even if Rydboholm is characterized by large-scale plantings, small additions, such as a circular granite bench creating a simple place to rest beneath a tree, can be very effective.

To create the feeling of an enclosed garden room, I planted a curved row of Japanese magnolias (*M. kobus*), its shape echoed by two large beds. I gave these beds a border of low-growing catmint (*Nepeta* × *faassenii* 'Cat's Meow') and filled them with old-fashioned pink and white shrub roses and transplanted peonies, with pale yellow rambling roses growing up custom-made pillars.

The central part of the flower garden is filled with perennials planted in lines and blocks to give the feeling of a summer meadow. There are also David Austin roses and giant feather grass (*Stipa gigantea*), as well as individual standard serviceberries trained into umbrella shapes, to provide a little shade and create the conditions for planting compositions of a different character.

The meadow around the moat

Around the moat we re-created low carpets of meadow with daisies (*Bellis perennis*), cowslips (*Primula veris*) and my favourite: germander speedwell (*Veronica chamaedrys*). Excess water from the moat flows into a stream and onwards into low-lying meadows. We planted Caucasian wingnut (*Pterocarya fraxinifolia*), red filbert (*Corylus avellana* 'Fuscorubra'), Turkish hazel (*C. colurna*) and pin oak (*Quercus palustris*) in the damp ground. I made the most of the moist conditions by planting large quantities of spring bulbs that would naturalize over time, primarily the narcissus varieties 'Actaea' and 'Recurvus', glory-of-the-snow (*Scilla forbesii*) and snake's-head fritillaries (*Fritillaria meleagris*). There was also a protected area of very wet marsh, which goes by the name 'Africa'. When the snow melts in the spring, snowdrops bloom in such quantities that they must have been growing there for more than 100 years. There is a strong and magical contrast between the untouched and the maintained land.

ABOVE A sea of wild blue phlox is backed by dark-leaved heuchera and Siberian bugloss.

OPPOSITE *Rhododendron dauricum* 'April Snow', an unusual cultivar with simple, airy white flowers, is planted among white woodruff (not yet in bloom), blue lungwort and white-flowered Siberian bugloss.

The area close to the castle

During the course of our work around the castle, we found beneath the lawns the remains of old tracks that followed the rocks and gentle undulations of the land in a natural way. We felt it was essential to reinstate these, since they told everyday stories of how people worked in the past. And, as we exposed as much as possible of the granite blocks close to the castle, it became clear how carefully the site had been chosen.

The castle, with its pinnacles and towers, was originally built on a rocky outcrop, surrounded by walls and moats in a relatively protected position. The pinnacles, towers and walls are long gone, and have given way to large flowerbeds along the western facade. Espaliered crab apples and pearlbush (*Exochorda* 'The Bride'), with their sparkling white buds and flowers, stand out against the rust-red facade. In the spring the beds are full of flowering bulbs, and in early June they are planted with summer annuals, in new combinations each year.

Woodland

To the west of the castle there were excellent conditions for a large area of woodland to which I planned to give definite winter and spring character. From the very start of the year the white flowers of *Viburnum farreri* fill the air with scent, making a simple yet effective combination with the coppery stems of dogwood (*Cornus sanguinea* 'Winter Flame'). The ragged yellow flowers of witch hazel (*Hamamelis* × *intermedia* 'Westerstede') appear at the same time, and spring in the woodland is crowned by the teardrop-shaped white flowers of the Carolina silverbell (*Halesia carolina*).

Early summer makes its grand entrance with the white blossom of the forked viburnum (*Viburnum furcatum*), while at the same time the elegant branches of the wedding-cake tree (*Cornus controversa*) burst into flower. Together with the katsura tree (*Cercidiphyllum japonicum*), this provides delightful spring foliage. The seven-son flower (*Heptacodium miconioides*) is a favourite of mine and of the insects, an autumn-flowering shrub with attractive flaking bark.

A flowering carpet

The woodland is underplanted with large, continuous areas of relatively simple plants, which give character and many wonderful

How wonderful it must be for the old lime tree to get a blanket of spring flowers beneath its canopy so late in life! Narcissi and wild blue phlox grow on a bed of different shades of green, and in the background is the white-flowered *Rhododendron* 'Cunningham's White'.

A Castle
B Courtyard
C Lake parterre
D Reconstructed terraces and walls
E Restored jetty
F Old rose garden
G Reconstructed lime avenue
H Avenue of Sighs
I The Brahe Monument
J The Countess's garden/ Baroque garden
K Island parterre
L Woodland
M Carp pond, remains of old moat
N Remains of moat around island
O Kyrkviken
P Orangery
Q Estate office

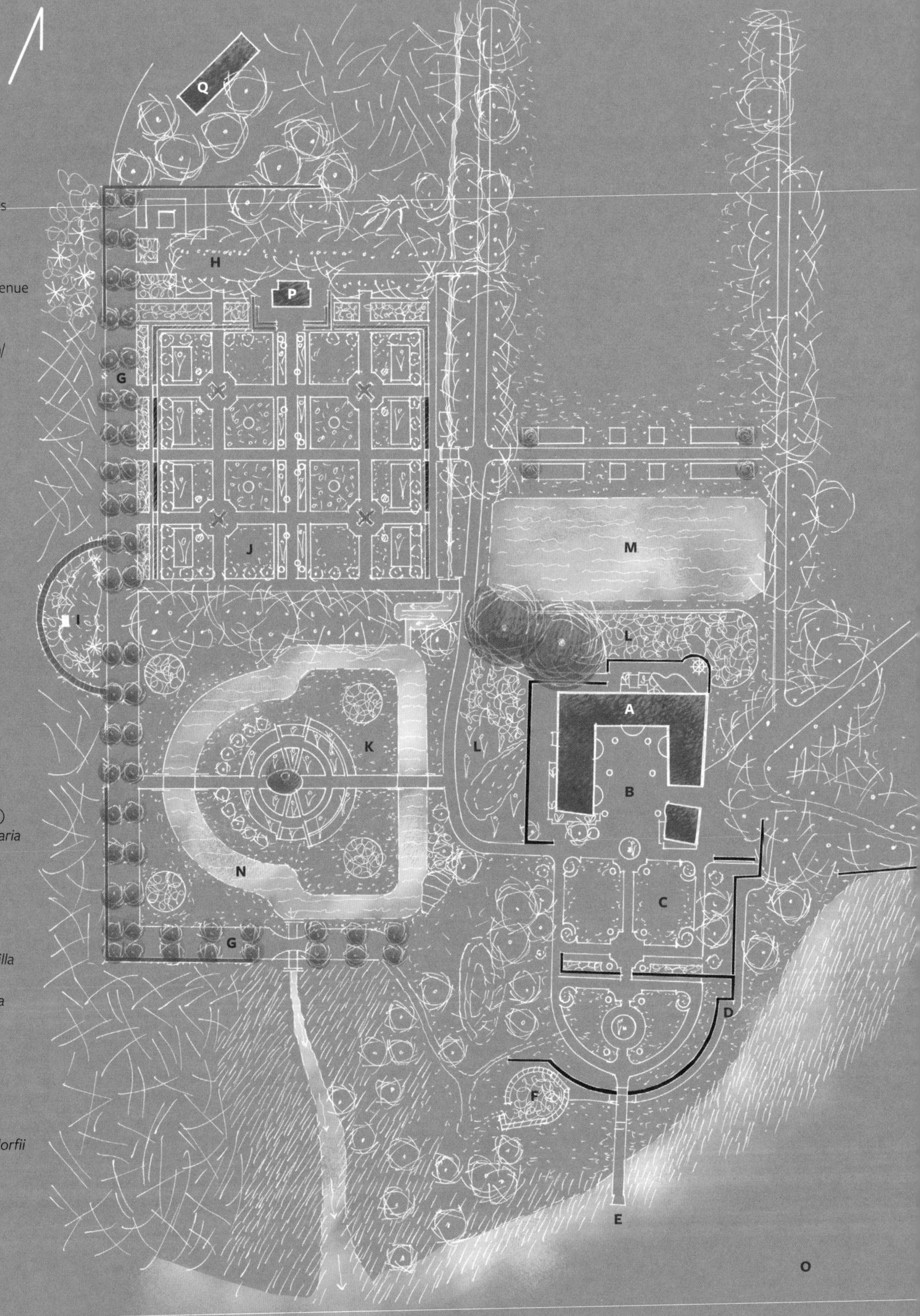

1 Cowslip (*Primula veris*)
2 Crown imperial (*Fritillaria imperialis* 'Rubra')
3 Snake's-head fritillary (*Fritillaria meleagris*)
4 Creeping navelwort (*Omphalodes verna*)
5 Pasque flower (*Pulsatilla vulgaris*)
6 Lungwort (*Pulmonaria* 'Blue Ensign')
7 Bearded iris (*Iris × germanica*)
8 Geum (*Geum* 'Scarlet Tempest')
9 Camassia (*Camassia leichtlinii* subsp. *suksdorfii* 'Caerulea')

1

2

3

4

5

6

7

8

9

BELOW In narrow beds by the castle is a cascade of lily-flowered tulips: orange 'Lilyfire', dark red 'Lasting Love' and 'White Triumphator'.

OPPOSITE Mercury looks out across Kyrkviken in a sea of fragrant tulips: the pink 'Angelique', maroon 'Uncle Tom' and white 'Mount Tacoma'.

colour combinations. It feels very special to see the early white *Rhododendron dauricum* 'April Snow' flowering at the same time as the narrow-leaved blue lungwort (*Pulmonaria* 'Blue Ensign'), white Siberian bugloss (*Brunnera macrophylla* 'Betty Bowring') and expanses of white sweet woodruff (*Galium odoratum*).

Spring-flowering carpets of blue and white phlox (*Phlox divaricata* 'Clouds of Perfume' and 'White Perfume') also provide a long flowering season in the bright partial shade.

The elegant combination of Himalayan blue poppies (*Meconopsis baileyi* syn. *betonicifolia*) and bright yellow lupins (*Lupinus* × *regalis* 'Chandelier') really does seem to glow when they flower beneath the trees. The same is true of ice-blue *Amsonia* 'Blue Ice' and blue Siberian bugloss (*Brunnera macrophylla* 'Jack Frost'), the white-streaked leaves of which are very effective alongside the dark-leaved *Heuchera* 'Obsidian'.

Late summer brings a restrained combination of pale green Japanese forest grass (*Hakonechloa macra*) and anemones (*Anemone* Ruffled Swan 'Macane007'[PBR]). The woodland continues to the north of the castle, with rhododendrons framed by granite walls leading down to the old carp pond.

The large rectangular lawn beside the pond, with its backdrop of old oak trees, has been supplemented with a parterre of yew hedges filled with transplanted white 'Iceberg' shrub roses. To give height to the parterre, I included some large specimens of clipped Norway spruce (*Picea abies*) – a particularly impressive focus for the eyes.

Time travel

My ambition is for the park at Rydboholm to give an experience of influences from the Renaissance, the Baroque and the English landscape style. It is my hope that my work will be seen as taking a humble approach to this historic site. The reconstructions, upgrades and new concepts that have changed the whole must shine through.

By adding a sense of nature, I want to emphasize the seasonal changes in my architectural style. What previously represented the slow development of the park over time –

PREVIOUS PAGES Sebastian Schildt's incomparable sundial shimmers with its Venetian gold mosaic, framed by gently shaped lawns with Baroque swirls at the corners, inspired by an illustration showing the park at Rydboholm in 1801.

LEFT The steps leading between re-created terraces of local granite are crowned by wrought-iron handrails. On the upper terrace, box hedges and globes of pruned privet frame standard hydrangeas, which have been on show at Rydboholm since the early twentieth century, albeit in a different location.

OVERLEAF The central axis of the Baroque garden is bordered by mirrored beds interspersed with circular granite benches. In mid-July white speedwell (*Veronicastrum virginicum* 'Album') and pink-white *Phlox paniculata* 'Rosa Pastell' stand out. The axis ends at an orangery designed by the architect Annette Lindberg, partly framed by a pleached beech hedge. The space in front is filled each year with summer-flowering plants in terracotta pots, here white mandevilla and red banana. In the background are the limes of the ancient Avenue of Sighs.

On the island is a cobbled meeting point around an extremely beautiful serviceberry. Variegated Japanese forest grass softens and frames the surrounding beds of perennials, and high-crowned serviceberries and pruned globes of red-leaved *Berberis thunbergii* 'Atropurpurea' give the planting coherent structure.

As autumn approaches, the colours of the garden mature, enlivened by large-leaved New York asters, calamint, monkshood and the seed heads of miscanthus.

BELOW At 59° north, conifers (*Thuja occidentalis* 'Smaragd') clipped into cones work very well. A contrast is provided here by a background of fountain grass (*Miscanthus sinensis* 'Kleine Fontäne').

OPPOSITE Autumn colour is seen from the same vantage point as the arrival of spring on page 62.

the trees – can today take a shortcut thanks to specialized nurseries that supply large, well-grown shrubs and trees. This was a prerequisite for the transformation of the park at Rydboholm Castle in a short time. Through the addition of a rich variety of large trees and shrubs, the castle is once again surrounded by greenery, and basks in an atmosphere in which the changing of the seasons offers new experiences all year round.

Maintenance and management

As a result of their structure, which relied on clipped plants and strictly managed areas of open space, Baroque gardens were labour-intensive and required a great deal of resources.

Rydboholm will be no exception if it is to be maintained at its current high level in the future.

Those of us who worked on the garden have used historical knowledge in combination with modern technology to lay strong foundations for the development of the park. Well-constructed earthworks, walls and bridges have revived and renewed the shape and structure of the estate. To create the conditions for sustainability over time, we used specially formulated soil containing compost and biochar, which should give the trees, shrubs and perennials the best conditions in which to establish and grow. All the trees and shrubs were chosen based on their hardiness. The perennials are a modern addition that make it possible to compose beds with a wealth of detail, while also contributing to the biodiversity of the park.

For the entire project to be sustainable in the long term, I used simple, long-lasting materials, such as granite and steel, for all walls, seats and trellises. Steel strips around all the lawns and beds will ensure the survival of the structure.

The water from the small stream supplies the pond and moat, but water for irrigation comes from four boreholes and a desalination plant. A large underground control room facilitates the management of the water for the flowerbeds, but there is also an advanced system for reusing any excess irrigation water. The surplus from irrigation and rain runs back into underground tanks, and if those become full, it flows into the stream. The system, which was developed during the construction of the park, can be compared to the advanced techniques of the Baroque period, when natural pressure from higher levels was used to supply water to ponds and fountains.

Grass-cutting robots, steel edging instead of a requirement for manual trimming, and the selection of specially cloned trees to limit pruning are just a few of the ways in which modern technology can contribute to a historic

Autumn in the Baroque garden (seen in the light of a spring morning on pages 60–1). The last plants to flower are monkshood, great burnet and asters.

In the autumn sun, bright yellow lime trees frame the large lawn. In the foreground is the old carp pond and newly planted yew parterres filled with white 'Iceberg' roses and marked by cone-shaped conifers.

site. This extends to the bedding areas in front of the castle, the combinations of which can be changed from year to year.

The future

Alongside all the knowledge, experience and technology involved in the renovation, an aesthetic eye and skilled handiwork are essential to the future development of the park, and it is important that the staff are able to cover all areas. The Baroque garden is by its very nature as far as one can get from the natural ideal of the English park, but through this update it now stands for both beauty and biodiversity.

The estate will be well maintained for the foreseeable future. The paths in the English park will be renovated so that they can cope with more visitors, but the Baroque garden remains private, albeit accessible to professionals in various contexts.

My hope is that Gula Brunn (the Yellow Well) pavilion, which was built by Magnus Fredrik Brahe in the late eighteenth century, and where people once 'took the waters', can be resurrected. Some of the simple original drawings of the pavilion, which stood at the point where the paths of the Baroque garden and the English park meet, at the start of the Avenue of Sighs, have been preserved.

Now that the renewed park has been running for several years, it is possible to summarize the changes that have taken place. The knowledge and ambition of the gardeners at Rydboholm are laying the foundation for the care and use of the park by future generations. Thanks to the high quality both of the facilities that were built and of the materials and plants used, there have never been such good conditions for this care. By allowing the 'invisible hand of the eighteenth century' – the gardener – to have a renaissance and be made visible in the park, I want Rydboholm to set an example from a national perspective, as well as to future gardeners.

OPPOSITE The view towards Kyrkviken.

PAGE 92 When snow settles over the garden like a protective blanket it brings a sense of tranquillity, and the park takes on a completely different atmosphere. The brown leaves of the beech hedge and the dark clipped conifers stand out clearly as Christmas approaches.
Photograph: Yanan Li

PAGE 93 If such a thing were possible, the sundial sparkles even more when the snow has settled and the sun shines for brief, precious moments.
Photograph: Yanan Li

RYDBOHOLM 2020

PREVIOUS PAGES The gatekeepers of the island, clipped pillars of beech, stand guard over the approach.
Photograph: Yanan Li

RIGHT Reconstructed walls and jetties of granite from nearby quarries were built by local masons. The walls mark the end of the park on the shore of Kyrkviken, but the reeds and landscaped lawns reveal that at one time the water level was much higher.
Photograph: Yanan Li

PHOTOGRAPHY
LISEN STIBECK

Ekholmsnäs Manor

The revival of a slumbering idyll

Set in beautiful countryside alongside Kyrkviken is an old manor house with a park-like garden that was in dire need of restoration and renewal. The site became the joint project of photographer Lisen Stibeck and John Larsson.

Ekholmsnäs was built in the late eighteenth century and has had many owners in the intervening years. The manor nestles in a beautiful natural landscape with a view of bays and islands. Ancient oaks of the same vintage as the house bring both a feeling of age and warmth of atmosphere, and the place has a strong, genuine identity that is anchored in the changing light and shade. Yet the estate isn't far from the bustle of the big city.

In the late 1890s the manor was immortalized by Richard Bergh in the painting *Nordic Summer Evening*, now in the Gothenburg Museum of Art. Few artworks have succeeded so expressively in depicting the melancholy that lies in the soul of the Swedish people. The painting shows two people – the artist Prince Eugen and the singer Karin Pyk – looking out over Kyrkviken from the balcony of Ekholmsnäs on a typical Nordic summer's evening. The landscape depicted in the painting remains much the same today, and provides the prelude to this gardening adventure.

Climate

A defining feature of the climate at 59° north is the clear differentiation of the seasons: autumn with its sharp colours and high air, relatively snow-free winters, and short, intense springs, when blue and white anemones cover the hills. And then the bright summers, of course, when the meadow flowers are in bloom, and which we want never to end.

Much of this has already changed as a result of today's climate fluctuation. There is often a lack of snow, and summers can be both hot and wet. But each season is still unique – the flowers and the light are still there – even if the differences are not as striking as they once were.

For the photographer Lisen Stibeck, the shifting light of the seasons is essential. For this reason, she dreamed that the layout of the garden, with different rooms, structures and planting combinations, would reflect and enhance the light of the different seasons.

It was an interesting challenge for me, given that I am particularly interested in light

and shade in gardens. We – me as a landscape architect and Lisen as a photographer – wanted the same thing: to bring to the fore the changing light of each season.

Supplementing the existing mature trees with newly planted ones was a way of enhancing the interplay of light and shadow in both the short and the long term. The old maples in front of the main building, which filter the light softly through their crowns, were one of the site's most valuable assets, along with the surrounding open countryside and the proximity to the sea. It was essential both to bear these in mind and to emphasize them. It was also important that anything we added to the landscape should remain subordinate to the site so that the scenery was reinforced in a humble way.

The approach to the manor is equally important. The initial work was therefore to clarify the entrance to the main building. After studying the differences in level, I concluded that a courtyard should be separated from the lower-lying grove of trees closer to the entrance. The slope was replaced by a wall of Corten steel, which marked a sharp distinction between courtyard and grove. We marked the boundary by the main road with a new fence, in which are set tall wooden double gates inspired by the Zorn House in Dalarna. The gate and fence, together with the old and new trees, give a feeling of authenticity and tradition. Inside, the drive leads to the courtyard with its new pond in front of the impressive eighteenth-century entrance to the main building.

At limited cost, the manor house's history and character were enhanced with new broadleaf trees to replace those that had died over the years, and to balance out the frame provided by the remaining older trees. A weeping copper beech was planted inside the gates, both as a focal point and to enhance the perspective towards the main building.

Pleached hornbeams filter the light and frame the garden room outside the kitchen, while a carpet of scented narcissi catches the soft spring light.

RIGHT In the large perennial bed, tall white foxtail lilies flower after the daffodils have faded.

OPPOSITE The spring flowers are succeeded by purple moor grass, which produces dark seed heads towards the end of the summer. Intensely blue perennials, such as sea holly and Russian sage, together with the warm colours of coneflowers, add character and variety to the planting, while also acting as valuable subsidiary plants until well into the autumn.

The wings were supplemented by two small beds of perennials, each containing a Japanese magnolia (*Magnolia kobus*), and box hedges were planted on either side of the main entrance. But the courtyard needed a central focus, and that was provided by a pond with a sculpture by Carl Milles. Perhaps this need arose because the *Naiad* sculpture already existed, but it turned out to be a wonderful feature, a real focal point in front of the beautiful eighteenth-century building.

In the pond stands the statue *Naiad with Fish* by Carl Milles.

Interaction between inside and outside

At the same time as the garden project was under way, renovation work was being carried out inside the main building. This included moving the kitchen to the western side of the house to give it a better connection to the garden. The associated requirements included converting the existing terraces into a large outdoor seating area to the west, with evening sun and a direct connection to the kitchen. To the north, we constructed a terrace with a view of Kyrkviken.

The work that was being undertaken around the stable block and the adjoining paddock led me to create a more secluded garden room close to the main building. We planted a row of pleached hornbeams (*Carpinus betulus*) and a clipped hedge of Cornelian cherry (*Cornus mas*) both to provide shelter from the wind and to make the terrace more secluded. On the terrace, behind the double hedge, we planted squares of box and yew, replicating the signs of previous plantings. In the squares closest to the seating area I planted high-crowned 'Evereste' crab apples with narrow canopies. These squares are planted with bulbs in the spring, then with summer bedding, such as *Verbena bonariensis*. When the white blossom of the crab apples appears, the bulbs are at their most beautiful. It's a wonderful time of year.

I gave this defined garden room a floor of Norwegian Oppdal slate in shades of grey, with space both for seating areas and for smaller beds containing cut flowers and vegetables, framed with Corten steel.

Depth of perspective

To make the entire park more accessible and useable, I laid out two paths leading from the stable in such a way that they cross on the terrace by the house. One is narrow and intimate, passing beneath existing fruit trees to emphasize the soft character of the park. The other is broader, and wider at the start to extend the perspective away from the main building. It leads across a lawn with areas of rock that have, over the years, become rich in wild flowers that thrive in the harsh environment.

The narrow path continues through a planted area of woodland towards the water, and the existing meadow shimmers yellow with cowslips in the spring. Most of the shaded woodland was planted with carpets of periwinkle (*Vinca major*), which provides dark,

Once the daffodils have faded, purple moor grass takes over. Above it rise sea holly and Russian sage, which flower later in the summer. In the background is my favourite, Japanese forest grass, planted in large drifts.

Crisp monkshood shimmers after the first frost.

dramatic foliage beneath larger specimens of white-flowered forked viburnum (*Viburnum furcatum*) and witch hazel (*Hamamelis* × *intermedia* 'Westerstede').

On the lower part of the slope, the planting transitions into carpets of lungwort (*Pulmonaria* 'Blue Ensign'), woodruff (*Galium odoratum*) and red barrenwort (*Epimedium* × *rubrum*). To achieve greater variation in height and leaf structure, I also planted *Rodgersia pinnata* 'Chocolate Wings' and ferns, among them the sensitive fern (*Onoclea sensibilis*), royal fern (*Osmunda regalis*), shuttlecock fern (*Matteuccia struthiopteris*) and male fern (*Dryopteris filix-mas*). These are all classic, robust woodland plants that belong in cool, humus-rich summer conditions.

The meadows by the kitchen

The scale of a garden is always crucial. In a large, park-like garden I position complex plantings closest to the house because that's where you spend most of your time. The further you move from the building, the more important it is that the planting becomes simpler – yet simultaneously larger, to command attention. By the kitchen we followed the principles of the summer meadow, interspersing grass with bulbs and perennials, to give a clear character from early spring to late autumn.

In these early months, when everyone is yearning for change, white Christmas roses (*Helleborus niger*) flower, and shortly after that the ground is covered with old-fashioned narcissi (*Narcissus poeticus* 'Recurvus' and 'Actaea'). Their blooms are quite similar, and together they provide a delightful spring shimmer. They are followed by burgundy *Allium* 'Mercurius' and white foxtail lilies (*Eremurus* 'Joanna') the height of a person. At the same time the restrained spikes of purple moor grass (*Molinia caerulea* 'Edith Dudszus') reach towards the sky. The meadows are at their best when these dark leaves are interspersed with lavender-blue Russian sage (*Perovskia atriplicifolia* 'Blue Spire'), sea holly (*Eryngium planum*) and warm orange coneflowers (*Echinacea purpurea* 'Sundown').

Summer brings tall speedwell in both blue and white (*Veronicastrum virginicum* 'Album' and 'Lavendelturm'). The tall brown spires of these linger long into the winter, together with the seed heads of the coneflower.

The wing with the small garden

Alongside one of the wings we laid out a small garden in the English style, but designed in a contemporary way. It contains luxuriant beds of such classic garden plants as granny's bonnet, salvia, iris and peony. I chose deep blue *Aquilegia* 'Hensol Harebell', the violet-blue clary sage (*Salvia nemorosa* 'Caradonna') and white-edged blue irises (*Iris* 'Silver Edge'), all held together by groups of silver-leaved mugwort (*Artemisia stelleriana* 'Broughton Silver'). To make the planting a little more coherent throughout the season, I included large recurring patches of Japanese forest grass (*Hakonechloa macra*), achieved by planting many small plants together. In late summer the beds are dominated by white coneflowers (*Echinacea purpurea* 'White Swan').

In the bed closest to the house there are old-fashioned scented white peonies (*Paeonia lactiflora* 'Duchesse de Nemours'), followed by white speedwell interplanted with masterwort (*Astrantia major* 'Superstar' syn. 'White Giant'), a favourite with its large white flowers. These perennials give the bed height and a bright glow throughout, including the edging of goatsbeard (*Aruncus aethusifolius*). Through the laying of a slate path between the shorter and taller beds, and the conscious use of a limited number of repeated plants, the beds gain both depth and character, despite their limited area.

Art in the garden

The artistic family at Ekholmsnäs were also interested in the way carefully positioned sculptures can enrich and enhance the various garden rooms. A number of artworks have been placed in a setting that harmonizes with each individual object. For instance, the French artist André Masson's magnificent sculpture *Femme tourmentée* is positioned by the entrance, beneath the old oaks. The fountain sculpture,

Purple moor grass catches the frost and the light along the path that follows the topography of the site.

A Entrance
B Courtyard
C Grove
D Residence
E West terrace
F North terrace
G Woodland
H Cowslip meadow
I Estate office
J Paddock
K Tennis court
L Stable yard
M Eric Grate, *Aquilegia*
N Corten steel walls
O Fence

1 Shuttlecock fern (*Matteuccia struthiopteris*)
2 Crab apple (*Malus* 'Evereste')
3 Sea holly (*Eryngium planum*)
4 Seed heads of martagon lily (*Lilium martagon*)
5 Coneflower (*Echinacea purpurea*)
6 Japanese anemone (*Anemone × hybrida* 'Honorine Jobert')
7 Panicle hydrangea (*Hydrangea paniculata* 'Great Star')
8 Japanese snowball (*Viburnum plicatum* f. *tomentosum* 'Mariesii')
9 Aster (*Aster macrophyllum* 'Twilight')

1

2

3

4

5

6

7

8

9

'The light, in combination with the warm autumn colours, the first frost, winter darkness and burgeoning spring greenery in the soft early summer light, with plants that change, bud and fade depending on the season, is exactly what I wanted. Seeing the way the more romantic and park-like areas interact with one another has given the garden a mature feel and a balanced setting. To be able to follow the different stages each day in my garden has become balm for the soul. Over the years I have learned a lot about how plants interact with one another. It is poetry in the form of gardening.'

Lisen Stibeck

Straw-stiff speedwell and coneflowers give the garden character all winter.

ABOVE By far the largest work of art in the park is the twin sculpture *Aquilegia* by the Swedish artist Eric Grate. From its site overlooking the sea inlet, on the large lawn beneath the canopies of ancient trees, it lifts the whole garden.

Naiad with Fish by Carl Milles, in patinated bronze, crowns both the pond and the area in front of the main building. The entrance to the terrace, meanwhile, is marked by a work in stone by the German sculptor Ulrich Rückriem.

This grand approach can be applied even in small gardens. The most important thing is not to over-furnish, but rather to let the sculpture and the spaciousness of the garden decide. In a small garden, instead of a sculpture, it is even possible to use a solitary shrub or tree with a beautiful branch structure, blossom and autumn colour.

LEFT On the rare occasions when snow settles, the garden's structure of neat hedges and pleached trees stands out.

Gardens in the City

Cultivating both ground and roofs for biodiversity

These two gardens are small pearls in the heart of Stockholm. Here, in spite of the limited space, planting is used to create rooms, spaciousness, perspective – and simultaneously to welcome the changing seasons.

The city garden

You can't get more central in Stockholm than the district of Östermalm. The townhouse is impressive, and in as close to original condition as you could hope for. Designed by the architect Erik Lallerstedt and built just over 100 years ago, it has a magnificent facade that forms a background motif in the streetscape. The property is surrounded by the tall plastered walls that are typical of the district, but there is no trace of the original garden apart from one beautiful old chestnut tree. As a consequence, the creation of a new garden was extremely exciting and challenging in terms of both its construction and future maintenance.

A vision of light and volume

Because the small garden was overlooked by taller neighbouring properties, one of my starting points was to reduce visibility so that the family, with their two children and two dogs, would have some privacy. In a city garden, where limited spaces are shaped by walls, the interplay of light and shadow is an important consideration. My aim was to make the small garden appear larger, and I achieved this by using clipped shrubs, which take up less space than free-growing plants, and by focusing the planting around the walls. The chestnut tree, together with the mature trees in the neighbouring plot, already gave character and provided a valuable frame of greenery.

After undertaking careful studies of the sun's trajectory, the proposal slowly emerged. The first element was a row of pleached limes (*Tilia* × *europaea* 'Pallida') placed against the wall to the north; with their narrow, vertical crowns, they frame a south-facing seating area. To give this corner the feeling of an arbour, climbing hydrangeas were planted against the walls behind the limes. The morning sun is important, and so as not to shut it out, I planted espaliered shrubby trees against the wall to the east, the

OPPOSITE Specially made containers with hidden wheels and an irrigation system make it easy to rearrange the garden. The circular granite bench, however, cannot be moved. The tree is a serviceberry underplanted with moor grass (*Sesleria nitida*). In the foreground are violets, white grape hyacinths, narcissi and red primulas.

same height as the wall. These were the winter-flowering Cornelian cherry (*Cornus mas*) and spring-flowering ornamental crab apple (*Malus* 'Evereste'), both of which have a defined branch structure and foliage that stand out against the plastered wall.

A small garden can be made to look bigger in different ways. I chose to create different rooms – an entrance area and a more intimate garden room – by dividing the garden with a north–south row of pleached hornbeams (*Carpinus betulus*), their crowns shaped into cubes. A low clipped yew hedge was planted beneath the hornbeams. As a result, both rooms receive maximum light. The row of shaped trees and the low hedge beneath resemble theatre scenery, offering both depth and perspective. Inviting visitors in but not revealing the whole garden until they enter it creates interest and anticipation, regardless of the size of the garden.

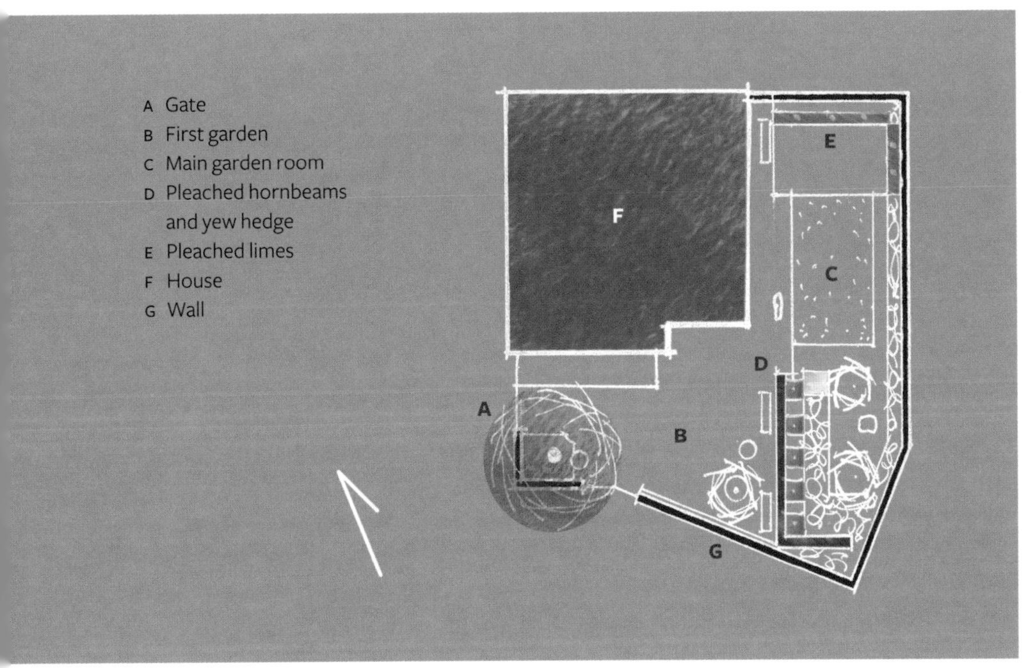

The entrance

The small entrance area consists of a hard surface of recycled slate and granite of different sizes and shades, the variety of which gives the impression of a carpet. The grand frame of the garden is made up of the row of hornbeams and a wall completely covered with the white-flowered *Clematis vitalba* 'Paul Farges' and a blue clematis (*C.* 'Jackmanii'). The wall is lined with flowering hostas (*Hosta* 'Patriot'), their variegated foliage catching the blooms of the clematis and giving a shimmering light to the paving in late summer.

Elegant covered steps bring historic character to the entrance courtyard. The site, which was intended for parking, developed over the years into a flower garden. Large steel containers with hidden wheels make it easy to rearrange according to season and requirements. In early March these contain spring bulbs, such as grape hyacinths and daffodils, followed by violets, primroses and forget-me-nots. In late April the multistemmed serviceberries (*Amelanchier lamarckii*) come into flower, their characteristic umbrella shape providing a roof for the flower garden; the trimmed hornbeams come into leaf at the same time. The composition provides several layers of blooms to mark the arrival of spring. When the summer comes, the containers are filled with annuals, which, as the season progresses, become more generous and convey a gentle suggestion of wild nature.

The inner garden room

In this part of the garden, two large serviceberries provide character. Their canopies filter the light and create playful shadows that help to balance the stricter language of the walls and the pruned elements. Their flowers are followed by those of espaliered crab apples.

The water in a small pond trickles restfully, linked directly to a bed containing perennials in various shades of green, interspersed with white, pale blue and pale pink flowers. The composition lifts the slightly shaded site. So that the serviceberries don't block too much light, their crowns are thinned each spring to provide as airy a structure as possible.

The contrast between the hard entrance and the softer green garden beyond remains strong throughout the summer. The facade of the house has been plastered in a shade of rust-red that brings warmth to the whole garden, while the garden walls are a sandy beige tone that creates harmony and balances light and shade.

In sunny spots the choice of plants is subordinated to the colour of the house, with the warm pink tones of rust-red species tulips (*Tulipa orphanidea* Whittallii group), pale pink tobacco plants in the summer and warm orange montbretia in the autumn. In shadier parts, the planting is white with elements of blue, to create a sense of coolness in the partially shaded garden. In the autumn the leaves on the cubes of hornbeam take on a rust-coloured tone, and the containers at the entrance to the garden are filled with flowers in the same colour range. As Christmas approaches, space is made for winter planting in green forest tones, often including white and pink Christmas roses. Above the seasonal variations, an elegant sculpture, *The Flower Vase* by the American artist Donald Baechler, catches the eye by the entrance.

Limited materials – slate, granite, gravel and steel – were used in the garden, with a variety of shaped trees and shrubs to provide an underlying structure that creates a framework for everyday family life. A small artificial lawn is a concession to the family's two dogs, which loved the real lawn literally to death. This is the first time I've used artificial grass in a private garden, and I must admit that the result looks fantastic, even if it really isn't environmentally defensible. The finishing touch is a large bronze sculpture shaped like a giant dice, *The Winner Takes It All* by Andreas Wargenbrant.

LEFT The row of hornbeams, the serviceberries and the red *Physocarpus opulifolius* 'Diable D'Or' glint in the spring sunshine. The shadows on the ground reveal that the photograph was taken in the middle of the day, demonstrating that the trees were carefully sited so as to cast the least possible shade on the garden. The large sculptures, *The Flower Vase* and *The Winner Takes It All*, contrast with the artificial but practical lawn.

BELOW Copper-coloured species tulips and narcissi.

RIGHT Spring planting in the specially made containers is in keeping with the beautiful building: Japanese maple and coppery wallflowers, with narcissi and white grape hyacinths.

OPPOSITE The small reflecting pond, trimmed yew hedge, gravel and granite catch the light beneath the tree. Here we see the verdant growth at the height of summer, with royal ferns (*Osmunda regalis*) and white masterwort (*Astrantia major* 'Superstar' syn. 'White Giant'), followed by Chinese meadow rue (*Thalictrum delavayi* 'Splendide White') and monkshood (*Aconitum carmichaelii*).

OPPOSITE Summer growth covers the trellises. A neatly trimmed yew hedge separates the hard entrance courtyard from the leafy part of the garden.

It is an honour to be able to follow a project over such a long time – ten years – in dialogue with the client and the maintenance team led by Ia Schildt. Sharing the experience gained also makes it a highly educational process, made possible by the team that cares for and maintains the garden.

Part of the natural development of a garden is the fact that the trees and bushes grow, and thus the light and planting conditions change. This in turn means that the planting gradually changes, with reduced flowering as a result. For this reason we have introduced ferns and other shade-loving plants, and the pruning of the trees and shrubs has become increasingly important in order to maintain the balance between light and shade.

The roof garden

As the city grows, gardens in the traditional sense are becoming increasingly rare, their place taken by balconies and terraces. The interaction between outside and inside makes this form of living attractive, and there are plenty of opportunities for variety, since garden rooms can be furnished according to mood and taste. Large terraces require as much planning as a garden, but also develop the living space to completely new levels. Growing plants on roofs, balconies and terraces is becoming increasingly common, and helps to contribute to biodiversity in our urban centres.

The roof garden (overleaf) has several terraces at different levels, which borrow some of the content and design of a garden. Tailor-

RIGHT An inviting dining area was created in front of a framework of pleached limes. The climbing hydrangea on the wall that surrounds the garden gives the feeling of an arbour, with limited oversight from the neighbouring buildings.

made solutions have been found, and there was also an ambition to create a rich environment for bees and butterflies, despite the small area.

The lower terrace connects to the social areas of the apartment, and has a dining area outside the kitchen framed by stagshorn sumac (*Rhus typhina*), followed by a long pergola walkway along the building. The pergola, with its specially made beams, provides support for climbing hydrangea (*Hydrangea petiolaris*) and *Wisteria sinensis* 'Prolific'. Between the uprights of the pergola there are round black containers of elegant katsura trees (*Cercidiphyllum japonicum*), which are beautiful all year round, with their silvery stems and buds in the spring, followed by handsome green foliage. Stockholm city centre forms the backdrop.

On the upper terrace we made a long steel container for perennials, where the choice of plants provides variety that enhances the seasons and brings a sense of nature amid the hubbub of the city. Spring and summer start with tulips, purple cow parsley (*Anthriscus sylvestris* 'Ravenswing') and bright red *Geum* 'Fiery Tempest', interspersed with trailing *Phlox divaricata* 'Clouds of Perfume'. At the height of summer the planting is dominated by Japanese forest grass (*Hakonechloa macra*), which gives the terrace character when its leaves move in the wind. Purple clary sage (*Salvia nemorosa* 'Caradonna') and double white yarrow (*Achillea ptarmica* var. *multiplex* 'Boule de Neige') give vibrancy to the planting in the summer, while the autumn gains colour and character from stonecrop (*Hylotelephium* 'Jose Aubergine'), white pearly everlasting (*Anaphalis triplinervis*) and blue scabious (*Scabiosa caucasica* 'Perfecta Blue').

Terraces are exposed to wind, sun and shade, and plants must be chosen with this in mind. But through the use of capacious planters equipped with simple built-in irrigation systems, terraces and balconies – regardless of size – can provide both variety and a foundation for good development over many years based on a manageable level of maintenance. It also helps to use moveable containers on wheels. Access to water and nutrients in the containers means that the plants grow more slowly, which helps to create planting that is sustainable over time.

OPPOSITE The pergola walkway, its black steel softened by the foliage and spring flowers of climbing hydrangeas, frames a view of the city.

ABOVE Perennials and grasses inhabit interconnected containers with built-in drip-irrigation. Japanese forest grass gives volume and character. In midsummer the prominent plants are clary sage and double white yarrow.

Villa Norrnäs

A shared vision

In an archipelago setting exposed to wind and weather, not far from the centre of Stockholm, a garden in dialogue with the surrounding landscape and the changing seasons has been refined to enhance the local climate.

The road to Värmdö passes through a dreamlike landscape, skirting fields and weaving its way past old oaks and gently undulating forested hillsides. Shallow inlets glitter along the way, occasionally hidden from view by patches of dense forest. As you arrive at Villa Norrnäs, a pastoral agricultural landscape opens up, surrounded by grazing deer and a wealth of birdlife. An oak gate covered by copper sheet with a perforated design of oak leaves is set in a tall wall of Nordic granite and provides a stylish entrance to this captivating Uppland setting.

Around the entrance, which leads down to handsome buildings designed by the architect Hans Blomqvist, a forested hillside with a carpet of sweet spring flowers spreads out. The two houses have been sited as they would have been in the past – subordinate to the landscape – which means that they do not compete with their surroundings. They share the same architecture, with curved roofs covered with attractive and functional carpets of stonecrop, so that they mirror the flora and granite outcrops of the landscape. In the background the wooded islands that mark the entrance to Stockholm harbour can be seen. It was into this natural scene – which hasn't changed for thousands of years – that I carefully inserted the garden.

Two families, one solution

It is unusual to find a relatively untouched landscape so close to a big city. Inserting a garden into this most beautiful archipelago setting requires a great deal of humility. I feel great respect for the surrounding landscape, a mixed forest of old ash trees, oaks and hazels that has an irreplaceable character.

The grassy terrain, with plenty of rocky outcrops, is rich with anemones and cowslips interspersed with all manner of ferns. I left the natural flora untouched and designed the garden to occupy the reclaimed land below the houses. Two families share the common space. It might be hard to imagine how the occupants

ABOVE The old oak hillside has a spring flora of cowslips and anemones.

OPPOSITE By the entrance, the preserved natural flora contrasts with the hard surface of granite slabs and cobbles in front of the houses. Granite slabs lead down to the garden through a reflecting pond and a moss-like bed of barren strawberry.

could agree on a garden with no hedges, walls or fences, and indeed creating a garden for two families in separate houses certainly required a great deal of consensus. At the same time, the size of the site gave the opportunity to create a common overarching solution with space for variation personal to each house.

Large spaces and intimate rooms

From the entrance gate, the garden can be described as a series of events, starting with the natural landscape. We move through the native flora that I love, and it is only when we reach a paved area in front of the two houses that the garden begins. The architect left a narrow passage between the houses, and this provides an effective sight line down to the garden and the sea beyond. From the entrance to the lawn, the garden drops by 6 metres. The large lawn gives a pleasant sense of being a communal picnic blanket, surrounded by clear scenographic elements. The design is based on a strict symmetrical framework that clearly leads down to the shore, and provides effective contrasts to the soft forms of the surrounding landscape.

Most of the planting close to the lawn is low, while rows of fastigiate oak (*Quercus robur* 'Koster') and willow-leaved pear (*Pyrus salicifolia*) standards provide height and frame the long sides of the garden. These beds have been given partially different characters to create contrast and variety. An imagined central axis across the lawn leads down to the shore and provides an open view between the two guest houses. Previously, reeds grew there on floodplains, but I have replaced these with beds of feather reed grass (*Calamagrostis* × *acutiflora* 'Karl Foerster') interplanted with Himalayan birch (*Betula utilis* var. *jacquemontii*). Large wooden decks along the entire shoreline frame the reed grass and provide plenty of space to enjoy the sun and the jetty.

Private rooms

The total size of the plot is approximately 10,000 square metres, which allows for various garden rooms of a more private nature close to the houses. By the eastern house, shaped dwarf Scots pines (*Pinus sylvestris* 'Watereri'), crab apples (*Malus toringo* var. *sargentii* 'Eskilstuna') and espaliered pearlbush (*Exochorda* 'The Bride') help to visually embed a large granite terrace. Beside the terrace I chose to create a stylized archipelago landscape using granite recycled from my *Daily Telegraph* garden at the Chelsea Flower Show in 2009. The range of plants goes from white and ice-blue to tones of black-blue from spring to late summer, and

includes violets, irises, clary sage, mullein and ornamental grasses.

On the eastern side of the garden there was a desire to create a small fruit and kitchen garden. In a formal garden, such an area must use a design language similar to that of the rest of the garden in order to maintain the overall impression. And, of course, a kitchen garden also requires careful positioning in terms of sun and protection from wind.

A fruit garden containing raspberries and both wild and cultivated strawberries leads to the kitchen garden, which is surrounded by privet hedging but open to the south to

Views from the entrance (opposite) and the garden (below). Fastigiate oaks enhance the central axis, embedded in carpets of barren strawberry.

Espaliered hornbeam hides the facade of the house and makes the lower floor part of the garden. In the foreground are the silvery seed heads of moor grass, with camassias and flowering crab apples.

capture the heat of the sun. Salad greens, Asian vegetables and more are grown in raised beds made of durable larch wood. An open bed contains potatoes, asparagus and currants.

Beside the kitchen garden is a partially open glazed room that provides a little shelter, although not so much as a greenhouse. Here I created the perfect place for tender plants – hybrid blackberries, kiwis and espaliered peaches, for instance – but without the problems (of pests and temperature) that are often associated with enclosed greenhouses.

Flowerbeds

On the western side of the central lawn I laid out large beds, protected by a tall, trimmed hedge of hornbeam (*Carpinus betulus*), which provides a classic element. The intention was to make the most of the local climate and allow the cultivation of as large a range of plants as possible. In the shelter of the hedge grow rows of free-standing fastigiate oaks and willow-leaved pear, and further in is a raised row of loosely shaped sea buckthorn (*Hippophae rhamnoides* 'Hikul') interspersed with Russian olive (*Elaeagnus angustifolia*) and serviceberry (*Amelanchier lamarckii* cv. Ultuna).

These are followed by a border in which silvery-grey moor grass (*Sesleria nitida*) is mixed with *Camassia leichtlinii* subsp. *suksdorfii* 'Caerulea' and *Narcissus poeticus* 'Actaea'. The cool tones of spring contrast with the warmer hues of summer, with red Japanese quince (*Chaenomeles* × *superba* 'Crimson and Gold'), purple-leaved smoke bush (*Cotinus coggygria* 'Royal Purple') and spurge (*Euphorbia griffithii* 'Fireglow'), interplanted with red-brown *Iris* Germanica group 'Natchez Trace' and copper-coloured species tulips, which give the bed a dramatic character and variety of colour.

High summer brings the abundant flowers of the butterfly bush (*Buddleja alternifolia* 'Nanhoe Blue'), bright blue Russian sage (*Perovskia atriplicifolia* 'Little Spire'), rust-red coneflowers, fiery montbretia (*Crocosmia* 'Lucifer') and white speedwell (*Veronicastrum virginicum* 'Album'), which links back to the colour palette of spring. Shaped dwarf Scots pines are used again here, to break up the planting. They give structure and winter character to the beds, and are underplanted with knotweed (*Bistorta affinis* 'Darjeeling Red'), among other plants.

OPPOSITE By visually inviting the natural landscape in, the garden gains perspective and appears larger than it really is.

ABOVE An effective composition of red-leaved smoke bush and Japanese quince, with the silvery tones of sea buckthorn, moor grass and dwarf Scots pine, is underplanted with camassias.

A Gate and drive
B Preserved natural area
C Garden entrance
D Buildings
E Rock garden
F Kitchen garden
G Perennial beds
H Wooden decking
I Glasshouse

EARLY SUMMER FLOWERS

1 Amsonia (*Amsonia* 'Blue Ice')
2 Species tulip (*Tulipa orphanidea* Whittallii group)
3 Cowslip (*Primula veris*)
4 Japanese quince (*Chaenomeles × superba* 'Crimson and Gold')
5 Narcissus (*Narcissus* 'Thalia')
6 Moor grass (*Sesleria nitida*)
7 Crab apple (*Malus toringo* var. *sargentii* 'Eskilstuna')
8 Camassia (*Camassia leichtlinii* subsp. *suksdorfii* 'Caerulea')
9 Smoke bush (*Cotinus coggygria* 'Royal Purple')

1

2

3

4

5

6

7

8

9

The stems of giant feather grass (*Stipa gigantea*) and round-headed garlic (*Allium sphaerocephalon*) add drama to the foliage of irises, sea kale and lavender – all surrounded by heavy granite slabs and dwarf Scots pine.

ABOVE Rambling roses grow on specially constructed pergola arches.

OPPOSITE The graphic elements are clearly visible: slate, gravel, grass and beds demarcated with steel strips. Clipped privet frames the small kitchen garden, where vegetables are grown in custom-made raised beds of larch. Peach and kiwi are among the plants growing inside the glazed cube.

Framing

To east and west the garden ends with clematis-covered colonnades with beds beyond. In the eastern bed, umbrella-shaped serviceberries are interspersed with (among others) apple trees, which give height. Here, too, a wide bed of pruned sea buckthorn, larger sea buckthorn and Russian olive stands in front of a row of fastigiate oak and standard willow-leaved pear. These form a kind of woodland edge that blends into the surrounding forest. The visual interweaving of the silver-greys and greens is magnificent.

After ten years, the large plantings that frame the lawn have grown up and formed multilayered beds of shrubs, bushes and perennials. These give shade and perspective to the garden, but above all, harmony. Among the plants, short-lived perennials have disappeared, including varieties of coneflower and scabious. Trees and shrubs have developed well and assumed a more defined character, such as the dwarf Scots pines and low-cut carpets of firethorn (*Pyracantha* 'Anatolia'). The fastigiate oaks, crab apples, serviceberries, sea buckthorn and Russian olives are increasingly connecting the garden to the surrounding landscape.

Rocks and sea

I wanted to use Nordic granite and slate for all walkways, walls and benches, as a reflection of the soft contours of the granite in the surrounding archipelago landscape. A stream runs from the natural landscape by the entrance, and the water from it is saved in ponds and reused for irrigation. In the central axis between the houses, I proposed a formal pond with granite stepping stones and jets of water that make the surface ripple and reflect off the white walls nearby.

The pond forms the entrance to the garden, from which you arrive on a terrace surrounded by hornbeam hedges. Here the line of sight between the houses and the lower garden is at its clearest. I reconciled the considerable difference in level using simple sculptural walls and steps of solid granite, softened by carpets of barren strawberry (*Waldsteinia ternata*).

In the lower part of the garden, in front of the pool room, I laid out a sculptural flight

Paths of Norwegian Oppdal slate in slabs 20, 30 and 40 centimetres wide connect the rooms of the garden. Granite blocks – recycled from my *Daily Telegraph* garden at Chelsea in 2009 – appear to float.

1

2

3

4

5

6

7

8

9

Autumn brings saturated colours, lit up by the silver of the grasses' seed heads and the leaves of lamb's ear (*Stachys byzantina*).

AUTUMN FLOWERS

1 Griffith's spurge (*Euphorbia griffithii* 'Fireglow')
2 Coneflower (*Echinacea purpurea* 'Alba')
3 Russian sage (*Perovskia atriplicifolia* 'Blue Spire')
4 Faded coneflowers
5 Montbretia (*Crocosmia* 'Lucifer')
6 Barren strawberry (*Waldsteinia ternata*)
7 Silver grass (*Miscanthus sinensis* 'Kleine Fontäne')
8 Smoke bush (*Cotinus coggygria* 'Royal Purple')
9 Sea holly (*Eryngium giganteum*)

ABOVE The barren strawberry forms a magnificent red-brown blanket in the autumn in a warm, sunny position. At the same time the hornbeam hedges and fastigiate oaks turn yellow.

OPPOSITE Autumn colours are set off by silver-leaved lamb's ear, the seed heads of purple moor grass and low clipped hedges of dark green firethorn.

of steps using thick slabs of Norwegian slate, with creeping thyme and cobbles. Through the planting of expanses of clipped shrubs, such as firethorn and hornbeam, the differences in level between the facades of the terrace and the garden are conjured away. A large block of solid granite and an Antarctic beech (*Nothofagus antarctica*) give this small sunken garden a strong graphic impression against the pruned hornbeam hedge in the background.

The garden illumination, by the lighting architect Torbjörn Eliasson, emphasizes the structure and highlights individual trees and shrubs. It creates new visual spaces, axes and lines in the autumn and winter, and the use of ground-mounted uplighters means that there are few fixtures to disturb the eye.

Construction

Where the garden is today was previously a reed-covered wetland. For many years before the start of the project, the wetland was built up with infill layers, partly to stabilize the land and make the construction of a garden possible, and partly to prevent flooding in the future. The houses, on the other hand, are built on solid ground, beneath the ancient rock at the rear of the garden.

The garden was constructed on soil that has been brought in, and over the years it has demanded a large supply of organic compost that has yielded great results. The natural stream from the neighbouring fields soon became insufficient for irrigation, so today there is a desalination system for seawater that makes the garden self-sufficient in water for the built-in irrigation system in the planting areas. Modern watering systems, together with the steel strips that edge all the beds, make the maintenance and management of the garden reasonable. Today there is one head gardener, who takes care of the garden with external help, which bodes well for the future.

The next step is to turn part of the large lawn into a flower meadow. This is another step that will meld the garden more closely with its natural surroundings.

I still follow the development and maintenance of the garden after all these years, and have come to realize that it is a unique place.

LEFT Clipped pines and sea buckthorn create a contrast to free-growing shrubs with their clear structures and textures. Naturally pale tones of silver and grey emphasize the purple of the smoke bush.

OVERLEAF When autumn arrives, the sun lights up the silver grass (*Miscanthus sinensis* 'Kleine Fontäne'), which is in full bloom. The maples in the surrounding landscape provide vivid autumn colour.

Today it enfolds the buildings in a positive way that has also contributed to an improvement in the microclimate. The task of anchoring the buildings in their magnificent natural setting with the help of the structure of the garden has certainly been worth the effort involved.

Seasonal magic

Over the years the garden at Villa Norrnäs has blended into its site in the archipelago. When the preserved flora by the entrance is in bloom, there is nothing that can compete with the anemones, cowslips and other spring flowers that are nurtured so lovingly here.

The character of the garden changes dramatically through the seasons as the plants grow in height and spread. And when the expanse of tall, silver-shimmering miscanthus is in flower and the reeds by the shore stand as yellow as straw in the autumn, the garden reaches magnificent maturity. The plants glow in these intense colours as a closing fanfare, one that explodes in carpets of barren strawberries as the foliage turns copper-red in the dry, sunny south-facing location. In this landscaped garden, surrounded by the nature of the archipelago, magic has been created.

ABOVE Slate steps are framed by cobbles and woolly thyme (*Thymus pseudolanuginosus*).

OPPOSITE The garden meets the entrance to Stockholm harbour with white-stemmed Himalayan birch in a large bed of feather reed grass.

Villa Kyhl

Sea and summer in Österlen

The garden of Villa Kyhl stretches from forest to sea. The house and garden sit like a pearl, surrounded by coastal forest before the sand dunes and sea take over. In this delightfully unique garden, new planting enhances the climate and natural surroundings.

Österlen is in the southeast of Sweden, where the bountiful agricultural landscape is gently hilly, and where small, picturesque coastal communities are embedded in the natural environment. This area includes the protected landscape of Sandhammaren, which consists of large expanses of sand dune covered with vegetation, beside a wonderfully long beach of soft white sand that squeaks when you walk on it. Lyme grass and heather grow on the dunes, sheltered in many places by windswept native pines (*Pinus sylvestris*), and it is this vegetation that gives Sandhammaren its unique character. The climate there is the mildest in Sweden, with temperatures that usually stay above freezing even in the middle of winter, but the region is buffeted all year round by strong winds from the Baltic Sea.

Villa Kyhl lies not far from Sandhammaren, behind an improbably beautiful beach. The road to the house passes through farmland and occasional patches of dark alder (*Alnus glutinosa*) woodland. The surrounding forest consists mainly of pines, with groups of tall alder in damper areas. The rippling stream that creates the conditions for these moisture-loving trees passes through the garden and a grassy coastal woodland before it reaches the Baltic. Stream and sea meet in a way that means the erosion-prone coastal landscape is constantly changing.

It was early spring when I first visited Villa Kyhl, and there were large patches of spring snowflake (*Leucojum vernum*) flowering in the forest glades. It was love at first sight, for both the forest and the bright, open beachside setting. The natural surroundings offered me both an opportunity and a path to follow when it came to planning and creating a garden there. As far as possible, I always want to connect to the existing nature in order to complement and enhance its presence with my designs for a site. Here, a depiction of the changes in the surrounding environment, from thick forest to the open landscape closer to the sea, came to form the main thread of the garden.

To the left of the gravel path is the old alder forest, with wild meadow flowers in the foreground, including cow parsley. On the right are carpets of ivy with yew and cherry trees, and a privet hedge in the background.

The forest edge

The autumn after my first visit, a storm brought down many black alders close to what was planned to be the main building. This became an important starting point for re-creating a strong boundary for the forest, a way of healing the scars. I chose to plant trees that are native to this part of Sweden, such as wild cherry (*Prunus avium*), crab apple (*Malus sylvestris*), beech (*Fagus sylvatica*) and English oak (*Quercus robur*). A mixture of large trees and small, shrubby specimens created variety in volume and height, and a forest edge that protects both the garden and the wind-sensitive woodland.

A narrow path between the remaining trees gave me the idea for this new forest edge. By adding some small raised areas, I separated the garden from the public footpath that runs past it, and echoing the shape of the dunes made it possible to raise the planting areas and thus prevent the high water table from reaching the plants' roots. This new, gentle topography created a visual connection to the foreshore.

Early on, I chose to supplement the classic woodland with wild species and also some garden varieties, since the joy of winter- and spring-flowering trees that provide interest throughout the seasons cannot be overestimated. I took care to choose varieties with as natural an appearance as possible: different types of viburnum, crab apple, spindle, serviceberry and yew, and – to reinforce the forest edge – hedges of evergreen privet (*Ligustrum vulgare* var. *italicum* 'Atrovirens').

From the outset, I wanted to create a classic woodland with ground-covering perennials suited to shade. This was not possible, however, because of the maintenance it would require over such a large area. The solution was therefore to use ready-planted carpets of ivy (*Hedera helix*) and periwinkle (*Vinca major*), which meant I could cover the ground in the first season, and also contributed to conserving the moisture in the soil. This proved a success, and thus the focus could switch to the beds of perennials close to the main house. After five years the edge of the forest has developed into a multilayered range of plants, forming an excellent windbreak for the old trees behind, and a delight for birds and insects.

In early May the copper beech (*Fagus sylvatica* var. *purpurea*) comes into leaf above a carpet of ivy and barren strawberry (*Waldsteinia ternata*).

The forest edge, with local crab apples, beech, English oak and wild cherry, planted in various sizes and quantities to give a natural impression. A large copper beech provides variation in colour. In the background can be seen the tall crowns of the magnificent black alders. In the foreground is a carpet of barren strawberry, with ivy further back. The path is made of pine bark.

OPPOSITE The narrow path with its playfully soft line leads towards the edge of the forest behind the elevated planting area. All the edges are marked out with steel strips to make long-term maintenance easier.

The garden close to the house

The added topography around the New England-style buildings provided a soft, natural transition to the forest beyond. A diagonal path was laid across the driveway, where a narrow glazed passageway connects the main building and guesthouse. This path made the garden feel more generous, with greater depth. It links the designed garden with the natural landscape surrounding it, while simultaneously enhancing the contrast.

The position of the buildings protects the plants on the north side of the garden from strong winds from the sea. There I planted perennials: a border of Siberian bugloss (*Brunnera macrophylla* 'Betty Bowring'), followed by blue irises (*Iris* 'Silver Edge'), ferns, including the sensitive fern (*Onoclea sensibilis*) and royal fern (*Osmunda regalis*), and narcissi (*Narcissus poeticus*). These are succeeded at the height of summer by white masterwort (*Astrantia major* 'Superstar' syn. 'White Giant') and lavender-blue speedwell (*Veronicastrum virginicum* 'Lavendelturm'), among other perennials, along with tall Chinese silver grass (*Miscanthus sinensis* 'Gracillimus').

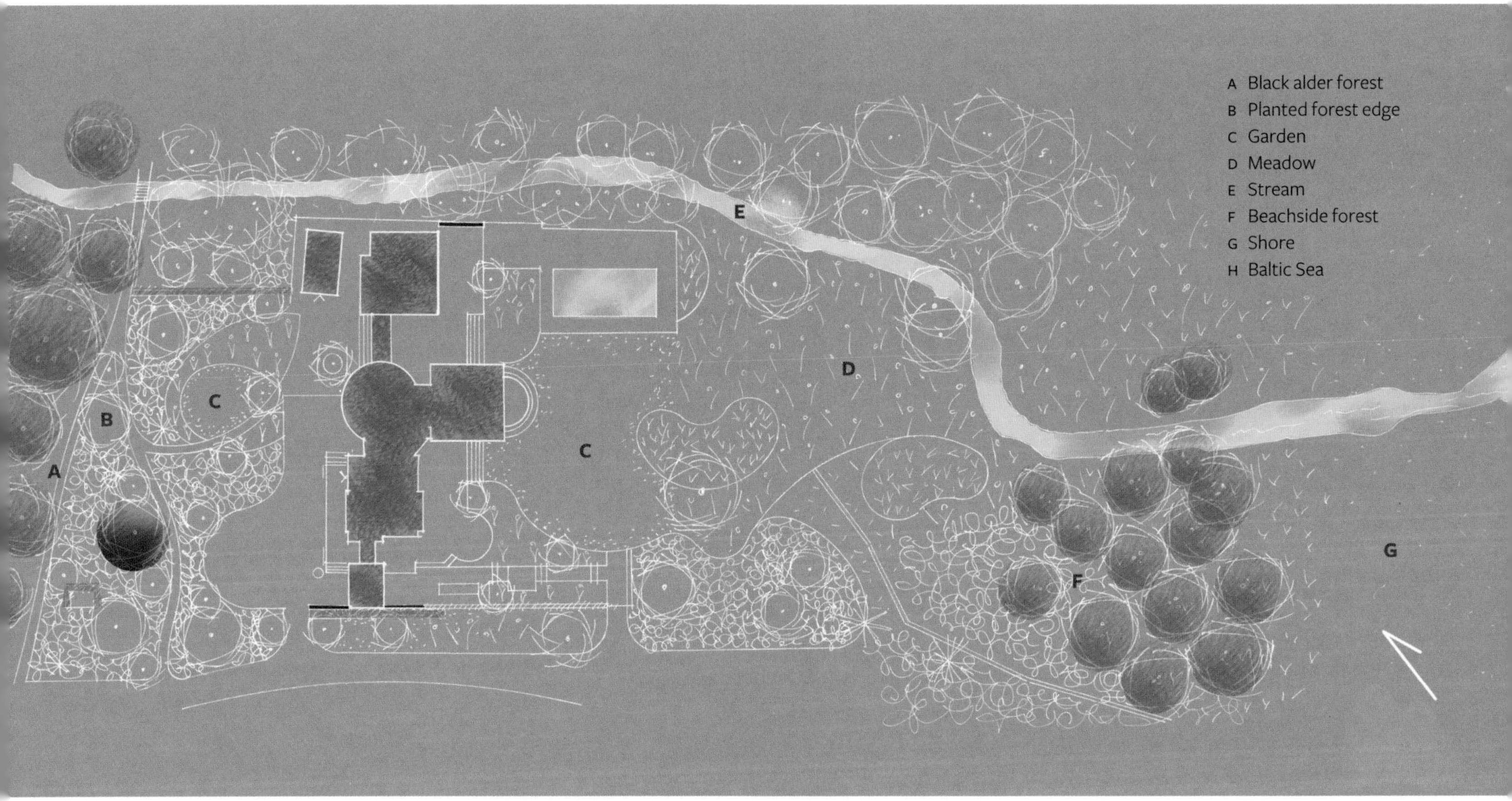

PREVIOUS PAGES In the foreground are blue and white Siberian bugloss and the foliage of masterwort, with royal and sensitive ferns.

RIGHT A sand-covered area exposed to the wind is planted with thrift, pasque flowers, thyme, moor grass, amsonia, clary sage, iris, calamint, Russian sage and low-growing, bright yellow Bokhara tulips.

OPPOSITE The bright shoots of the wedding-cake tree (*Cornus controversa*) with its horizontal branch structure, in a bed of perennials and thyme, are reflected in the pool in front of the guesthouse. Solid granite steps lead up to the south-facing terrace in front of the guesthouse, where I placed containers for seasonal plants. The lemon trees in their terracotta pots have just emerged from winter storage in the glazed linking passageway.

The planting is surrounded by umbrella-shaped serviceberry (*Amelanchier lamarckii*), which produces a profusion of white blossom in spring. There is also evergreen yew (*Taxus baccata*) and flat-stalked spindle (*Euonymus planipes*), but it is the pair of Kentucky coffee trees (*Gymnocladus dioicus*) that really lend the area an exclusive, airy character.

The garden by the sea

On the side facing the sea, the garden is concentrated in the areas closest to the buildings. The beds are covered with fine sand, which provides well-drained, warm surfaces and favourable growing conditions for plants with modest requirements. In early spring the pasque flowers (*Pulsatilla vulgaris*) and white thrift (*Armeria maritima* 'Alba') come into flower, interspersed with yellow tulips (*Tulipa linifolia* Batalinii group 'Bright Gem') and the soft spears of moor grass (*Sesleria nitida*), followed by blue scabious (*Scabiosa columbaria*). Irises of various kinds break up the simple composition. Later, at the height of summer, lavender, Russian sage (*Perovskia atriplicifolia* 'Blue Spire'), clary sage (*Salvia nemorosa* 'Caradonna'), calamint (*Calamintha nepeta* 'Blue Cloud') and *Amsonia* 'Blue Ice' all flower in different shades of blue.

A path of large, natural slabs of Norwegian slate leads through the planting, interplanted with wild thyme (*Thymus serphyllum*). It leads to a neatly trimmed privet hedge beside a rose-covered pergola. The hedge sets off the simple flowers and the opulence of the roses. Behind the pergola grow currant bushes, fruit trees, and wild and cultivated strawberries. This area is followed by a landscaped lawn, then a meadow of wild flowers that not only adds beauty in the summer, but also encourages biodiversity.

The garden spreads in a sweeping arc from forest to sea. By responding to the conditions of the landscape, I was able to create a garden that is close to nature and therefore requires only modest maintenance and care. However, the different areas require more knowledge and experience than a traditional garden. In a garden of this kind, which is close to nature, it also becomes clearer how the plants develop over the years. The freshly planted edge of the black alder forest has managed in a short time to establish a varied range of plants that was previously missing.

OPPOSITE Junipers and rhododendrons from the old garden – along with low-growing sea buckthorn bushes – were incorporated into the new garden, in front of the coastal woodland of pines and black alder.

ABOVE Freshwater meets seawater where the stream flows into the Baltic Sea.

RIGHT A path of oak planks echoes the terrain and links the shore with the house in an intentionally casual way; it is meant to look as if it has always been there. It passes existing expanses of beach roses (*Rosa rugosa*) and dyer's broom (*Genista tinctoria*). Both of these are invasive species, and in Österlen efforts are being made to eradicate them.

OPPOSITE Before the stream flows out into the sea, it passes a planted meadow beneath black alders. In early May cowslips predominate, closely followed by various wild flowers, including harebells, wild scabious and sheep's-bit. Several plants beloved of butterflies also grow here: daisies, bird's-foot trefoil and spiked speedwell, as well as saxifrage, wild pansies, sea campion, lady's bedstraw, sticky catchfly, heath speedwell and silverweed. This rich mixture of meadow flowers was planted as small plug plants.

Lund City Park

The garden of sunshine and shade

The entrance to Lund City Park is intended to conjure the feeling of walking through a flower meadow, from the first blooms of spring to the warm colours of autumn. The project encompassed a range of planting conditions, so a large palette of plants was used in various layers to create contrast, harmony and variety.

Lund University was founded in 1666, and has maintained its position as one of the foremost seats of learning in Sweden ever since. University life has always had a strong connection to the city park, and over the years the edges of the park have gained student facilities, such as swimming pools and sports halls. When the park was approaching its centenary in 2011, the City of Lund asked me to come up with a fresh development plan for its restoration and renewal, since it was looking rather tired. The objectives were to update it with new destinations and activities, to add more varied planting to provide greater seasonal variation and thereby to make the park attractive even in the winter, while simultaneously taking into account its historical and ecological significance.

As in all urban development, past and present meet here, and it was important for me as a designer to embrace that. A section of city ramparts dating back to the twelfth century – a national monument that is unique in the Nordic region – divides the park both visually and in functional terms, by forming a boundary for the new garden. In the late nineteenth century, when the park was being constructed, a summer restaurant was built, with a classical wrought-iron fountain close to the entrance. The fountain is still there to this day, and had to be taken into account. Several buildings also remain from the large exhibition of industry, handicrafts and art that took place in 1907, lending the park the character of a bygone era.

A number of different gardening styles meet at the centre of the park. These include formal elements inspired by the French Baroque, as well as beds designed along classical lines. Other areas have the character of an English landscape garden, with winding paths and ponds.

Beside the entrance is the gardener's residence, dating from the late nineteenth century, next to preserved greenhouses from the same period. Adjacent to the greenhouses there was once a large nursery for raising plants for the park, but this no longer exists. In the

The white flowers of Siberian bugloss and 'White Triumphator' tulips light up near-black 'Queen of Night' tulips and Persian lilies.

1990s the greenhouses were converted into aviaries. The large birdcages were embedded in trees with airy crowns, such as gleditsia and robinia, to give the area a natural feel. In front of the remains of the old horticultural workshop I was asked to create a destination for visitors in the form of a garden.

The idea

The transformation was named 'The Garden of Sunshine and Shade', and took as its starting point the garden associations that once existed in various parts of the country, often attached to urban parks. One of the reasons these parks were created was for the education of the public, and they became important sources of inspiration and knowledge about plant varieties and what people could grow in their own gardens. In Gothenburg and Linköping, these garden associations still exist, and they still fulfil an important function. The idea behind the initiative in Lund was to combine an interest in horticulture with architecture and design – all in an appealing environment and with a focus on plants, their composition and their cultivation.

My concept was inspired by the strict layout of the old nursery, with a grid of paths and raised beds. The new grid was created with the help of intersecting paths and regular access paths for maintenance. As a result, small meeting points arose, which I furnished with specially designed benches in wood, steel and granite, set on slate paving. The design language is contemporary, and contrasts with the restored wrought-iron fountain from the early years of the last century. A range of benches was placed around the fountain, framed by granite walls against the backdrop of large beds of perennials. The garden is surrounded by lawns, which have long been filled with a rich array of naturalized spring bulbs.

The park largely lacked winter- and spring-flowering shrubs and trees, so I consciously chose varieties with early flowers and autumn colour, qualities that enhance the changing of the seasons. Lund's location in the south of Sweden, with its mild winter climate and relatively long, warm summers, made it possible to use such species as the handkerchief tree (*Davidia involucrata* var. *vilmoriniana*), with its magnificent blossom in early summer, and the

The restored fountain is more than a century older than the bench that surrounds it. In the foreground is a specially designed circular granite bench beneath a Kentucky coffee tree, and in the background the old city rampart is visible.

The Garden of Sunshine and Shade is an addition to the site where the restored fountain stands, together with new benches in black glulam and stainless steel. At the turn of the last century it was surrounded by a large building selling refreshments. The 'Evereste' crab-apple trees contribute blossom in spring. Tulips in white and black enhance the scene, along with Persian lilies.

Creating structure in a park or garden is of the utmost importance. Planting neatly trimmed hedges is one way to frame a small area, create rooms and play with daylight.

Kentucky coffee tree (*Gymnocladus dioicus*), known for its airy, elegant crown. I also chose grasses and perennials that would give interest from early spring until well into the autumn.

Around the site of the fountain we removed some old, tired trees to let in more light and warmth. A large, stately, healthy beech with a broad crown remains, however, lending character and light shade.

The planting

Over the years I have explored many different ways of planting perennials. These days I like to plant several different layers, a model that works well for both strict and looser, more meadow-like plantings. This method can also be used to allow plants to enhance one another's characteristics, or to change the feel of a bed during the season. To make the maintenance of public displays more manageable, the

A Main entrance from city centre
B Former gardener's house
C Preserved greenhouses
D Preserved office buildings
E Aviaries
F Pond with wrought-iron fountain
G Seating area
H Beech tree
I Pleached hornbeam with privet hedge
J Perennials
K Old city rampart

The newly constructed part of the park is surrounded by lawns containing naturalized spring bulbs. It was an easy decision to plant a variety of tulips in different colour compositions in the perennial beds. In the south of Sweden, tulips can survive for several years before their strength begins to fade.

LATE-FLOWERING BULBS

Allium 'Gladiator' – ornamental onion, lavender-blue
Eremurus 'Brutus' – foxtail lily, white
Fritillaria persica – Persian lily
F. 'Chopin' – crown imperial, orange, dark-stemmed
Tulipa 'White Triumphator' – white, lily-flowered
T. 'Lilyfire' – orange-yellow, lily-flowered
T. 'Merlot' – burgundy, lily-flowered
T. 'Queen of Night' – brown-black
T. 'Havran' – brown-red
T. 'Request' – orange/brown

The avenue of pleached hornbeam forms the backdrop, while simultaneously segregating and providing new rooms for the old gardener's house and greenhouses. Mediterranean spurge (*Euphorbia characias* subsp. 'Wulfenii') forms impressive lime-green ridges in the perennial beds in the spring. It is not reliably hardy in cooler regions, but can be replaced with marsh spurge (*E. palustris*).

ABOVE A seed head of honey garlic (*Allium siculum*).

OPPOSITE A grid of slate-paved access paths is consistent throughout the garden, based on the layout of the plant nursery that once occupied the site.

number of different varieties must be kept to a reasonable level. This method can also be used in private gardens, large or small, and it is a good way to create personality, calm and harmony.

Two or three perennial varieties were planted in each rectangle of the grid. Some rectangles were reinforced with exclamation marks in the form of individual taller perennials and grasses. For some, I chose plants of similar height, while others contained varieties of differing heights. The combinations were varied by some plants recurring in several rectangles, while others were more specific to their location.

The keywords for the city park were variety and diversity, concepts that are valuable not least because the city is surrounded by an open agricultural landscape that is not easily accessible. The park therefore acts as a substitute for the nature to which the population lacks access. Trees and shrubs were planted to create smaller garden spaces, without casting too much shade over the beds.

The large beds of perennials were planted with quantities of spring bulbs, which, with the earliest perennials, create a display in shades of white, purple, pink and brownish-red, with touches of lime. In early summer, when the perennials are at their most vivid, the beds change rapidly in both growth and appearance. The colour scale shifts to a warmer yellow-red-orange in the southernmost part of the garden, and blue-violet in the shadier part. This culminates in July with further defined shifts in colour. Some plants, such as the salvias and catmint, are cut back after flowering to encourage a second flush of blooms.

As the summer progresses, the volume of plants grows and the seating areas become intimate islands between the beds. This is when the thickets of elephant grass (*Miscanthus sinensis* 'Purpurascens') fill the beds with their large plumes. In late summer tall plants, such as asters, bugbane, monkshood and various grasses, give the beds character. Autumn is enriched by plants that develop attractive, nut-coloured seed heads; to the delight of the birds, these are left over the winter and cut back only

in the spring. In the light shade of the remaining beech, I planted an expanse of Japanese forest grass (*Hakonechloa macra*), interspersed with white flowers.

Trees

The main entrance to the park was framed by small trees that blossom profusely in the spring, such as Japanese magnolia (*Magnolia kobus*), cone-shaped crab apple (*Malus* 'Evereste') and hawthorn (*Crataegus lavallei* 'Carrierei'). To create a clear backdrop for the new garden on the site of the old nursery, and to delineate a space in front of the old greenhouse, we planted a hedge of evergreen privet (*Ligustrum vulgare* var. *italicum* 'Atrovirens') and a row of pleached hornbeam (*Carpinus betulus*).

The path leading into the park is lined with handkerchief trees, and even if it takes many years for their flowers to appear, it will be worth the wait. The same goes for the slow-growing Kentucky coffee trees, which will form beautiful canopies with their framework of branches and lobed leaves. While waiting for the trees' characteristic shape and flowers, passers-by can enjoy the Chinese dogwood (*Cornus kousa* var. *chinensis*), which blooms happily the year after planting. Katsura (*Cercidiphyllum japonicum*) and red-stemmed dogwood (*Cornus sanguinea* 'Winter Flame') have been planted because their branches have such individuality in winter.

Specimen shrubs

For winter character, I planted early-flowering shrubs, such as the pink Farrer viburnum (*Viburnum farreri*), pale yellow witch hazel (*Hamamelis* × *intermedia* 'Pallida') and the orange variety ('Jelena'), as well as the Cornelian cherry (*Cornus mas*), which bears greenish-yellow flower clusters on bare stems.

The spring garden glows with pearlbush (*Exochorda* 'The Bride'), hybrid magnolia (*Magnolia* × *loebneri* 'Merrill'), forked viburnum

LEFT The light in a park or garden can be captured by the choice of plants. My high-summer favourite is the lemon-yellow daylily (*Hemerocallis citrina*), and the insects' favourite is white speedwell (*Veronicastrum virginicum* 'Album'), seen here with large mounds of Japanese forest grass and red elephant grass, which change the structure and height of the beds as the season progresses.

OVERLEAF The perennials are planted in groups, often with others of varying heights. Here red-brown *Helenium* 'Rubinzwerg' peers through in a bed that has been taken over by sea holly (*Eryngium giganteum*), which has self-seeded prolifically in just a few years. The Mediterranean spurge is also fascinating, because it rarely achieves the volume seen here. To the right is a bed of false indigo (*Baptisia australis*), which flowers early in the summer. In the foreground is another insects' favourite, catmint (*Nepeta* × *faassenii*), and in the background tall lavender-blue speedwell (*Veronicastrum virginicum* 'Lavendelturm'). On the left is one of the recurring cushions of Japanese forest grass.

(*Viburnum furcatum*) and Japanese snowball bush (*V. plicatum* 'Mariesii'). All contribute blossom in various shades of white until well into early summer.

As late summer and autumn approach, it is the hydrangeas (*Hydrangea paniculata* 'Great Star' and 'Kyushu') that are responsible for the floral display. By far the most beautiful is 'Great Star', with its large, wide-open flower clusters that look like dancing butterflies as dusk settles on the garden.

Grasses with character

To give the perennial beds structure and character, I used recurring groups of grasses. Japanese forest grass, which also forms a carpet beneath the large beech tree, appears in several places, while red elephant grass (*Miscanthus sinensis* 'Purpurascens') forms fountain-like clumps with shimmering silver seed heads and red autumn colour. Varying combinations of grasses and perennials occur throughout the garden, often including moor grass (*Sesleria nitida*), which produces silvery shoots in spring. At the height of summer, purple moor grass (*Molinia caerulea* 'Edith Dudszus') acquires its characteristic upright, stiff seed heads, while Korean feather reed grass (*Calamagrostis brachytricha*) produces its almost luminous silvery seed heads. The silhouettes of these grasses are of great value throughout the winter.

RIGHT Sea holly (*Eryngium giganteum*).

OPPOSITE In the foreground is calamint (*Calamintha nepeta* 'Blue Cloud'), with large groups of clary sage (*Salvia nemorosa* 'Caradonna'). The tree with the attractive bark and grand foliage is a Kentucky coffee tree. In the background are mounds of Japanese forest grass and red elephant grass.

PAGES 188–9 The Garden of Sunshine and Shade is separated from the buildings and greenhouses behind it by a row of pleached hornbeams, a hedge of evergreen privet and summer-flowering white hydrangeas (*Hydrangea paniculata* 'Great Star'). The beds are edged with low granite blocks. Here, cushions of Japanese forest grass are clearly visible, while the Chinese silver grass needs another month to grow and flower.

Villa La Moutte

A modern villa on the site of an old vineyard

In the South of France lies a garden that visually invites in the lush pine landscape that surrounds it. Here you can find garden rooms of varying character, where the choice of materials and colours is influenced by selected works of art.

Gentle winds, dark summer nights, olive trees, the smell of the Mediterranean and citrus trees: that, to me, sums up the landscape outside St-Tropez, close to the beautiful coastal landscape with its beaches and azure sea. This is where the gardening cultures of Sweden and France have been able to unite and reflect our time.

Inspiration

In 2011 Alexandra and Stéphanie de Nonancourt, owners of the great champagne house Laurent-Perrier, commissioned me to create a garden to commemorate the Royal Horticultural Society's centenary at the Chelsea Flower Show in 2013. It was far too tempting an offer to turn down, despite my experience of Chelsea 2009: several years of planning and hard work with an immovable deadline, but involving the sort of collaboration with knowledgeable people that I love.

Once I was in the Champagne region, where I received a warm reception at the chateau, my enthusiasm and interest were aroused – not only for the fine drink, but also for the way in which the landscape had been used for wine production, and how this craft had developed after the Second World War. I went away with the desire to combine an elegant garden for our time with a strong feeling for nature. That was all!

I immediately began to search for a connection between my design world and the French equivalent. The key to success at the Chelsea Flower Show is to tell a story, and to present it in a fabulous way. But everything I came up with felt tenuous and irrelevant. Then, one day, I received a tip from a journalist friend in France, Louisa Jones, about a different kind of garden: La Louve in Bonnieux, in the heart of Provence – a famous garden designed and built by Nicole de Vésian, chief designer for Hermès in Paris in the 1950s and 60s.

After contacting the owner, we were given the opportunity to visit the garden, which wasn't easy to find, being hidden behind high

A ceramic oxblood-red bull by Ulla and Gustav Kraitz grazes on a meadow of Chinese fountain grass. In the foreground is a striking ceramic lemon by Hans Hedberg.

ABOVE The entrance drive winds beneath old cork oaks and newly planted fastigiate oaks and hedges.

OPPOSITE The area by the pool house contains various forms of *Salvia*. Beneath the bird-of-paradise tree are shaped cushions of holly and privet. The rose is 'Pierre de Ronsard'.

walls on the village street. But when we finally found it, the garden blew us away. Vésier is an icon in France, and although she didn't work on many gardens, her designs are said to bridge the gap between classic, formal French gardens and informal modernism.

La Louve

The garden in Bonnieux is not large – about 500 square metres – and is set on a north-facing terrace with a view of the countryside. The work exudes self-confidence in its design, architecture and materials, combined with a wonderful simplicity that completes the experience.

Vésier's elegant design language is reflected in her ability to recycle and combine such materials as stone and wood with local plants that can cope with the climate. One of her signature features is hand-trimmed evergreen shapes, something that was unusual in garden design when La Louve was created in 1996. At the time of our visit, the garden was still intact thanks to the efforts of its owner, the art dealer Judith Pillsbury from Paris, and her two gardeners. Judith saw the garden as a work of art, and maintained and preserved it during her time as its owner, a humble and respectful act in a period marked by constant change.

The entrance to the garden is through an old stable, a stone building with a gravel floor. The darkness of the archway leads out into bright light, where you are met by terraces with different characters. Walls, steps and pavements are built from recycled stone of various types in charming patterns that build up the all-encompassing work of art the garden represents. Vésier used green foliage textures in carefully composed, often clipped compositions to create contrasts between light and shadow. She also had an outstanding ability to invite in the surrounding landscape below the terraces. Her lavender beds, in which every other row is cut early to promote flowers throughout the season, are world-famous.

Vésier's choice of local plants, such as lavender, cypress and other drought-resistant species, was far ahead of today's awareness of the changing Mediterranean climate. During my visit, I noticed a kinship with the design

PREVIOUS PAGES An exclusive collection of fruit by the ceramicist Hans Hedberg. The plum in the foreground is surrounded by dark purple irises ('Black Swan') and red kangaroo paw. The giant feather grass catches the light. In the background are globes of privet (*Ligustrum jonandrum*) and trellises covered with star jasmine (*Trachelospermum jasminoides*). On the right is a trimmed cypress hedge that acts as an extension of the stone wall. Against the hedge, white 'Iceberg' roses in both bush and standard forms are interspersed with a mass of Mexican fleabane, which flowers here all summer.

language of the Swedish garden designer Ulla Molin, and indeed the two were active at roughly the same time.

Molin – the founder of modern Swedish garden design, both as a designer and as a journalist – must have been to La Louve, I thought. The two designers share a humility towards the landscape and the strict construction of the structure of the garden, with restrained choices of simple plants, often in clipped forms. They even share a relationship with sun and shade in a way that could hardly be coincidence. Molin inhabited a world of form and design, and worked with the best Swedish architects, craftspeople and nurseries of the time. Her garden at Höganäs (1970) came to be seen as a masterpiece.

I consider myself very lucky to have been able to engage with the work of both these women: the limitless interaction between outside and inside, and their austere simplicity. It isn't that their gardens don't contain flowers, but primarily their aesthetic and functional creations unite two cultures, and this has left a clear impression on both France and Sweden. That came to be my inspiration for the Laurent-Perrier garden at Chelsea in 2013 – an almost unbelievable adventure.

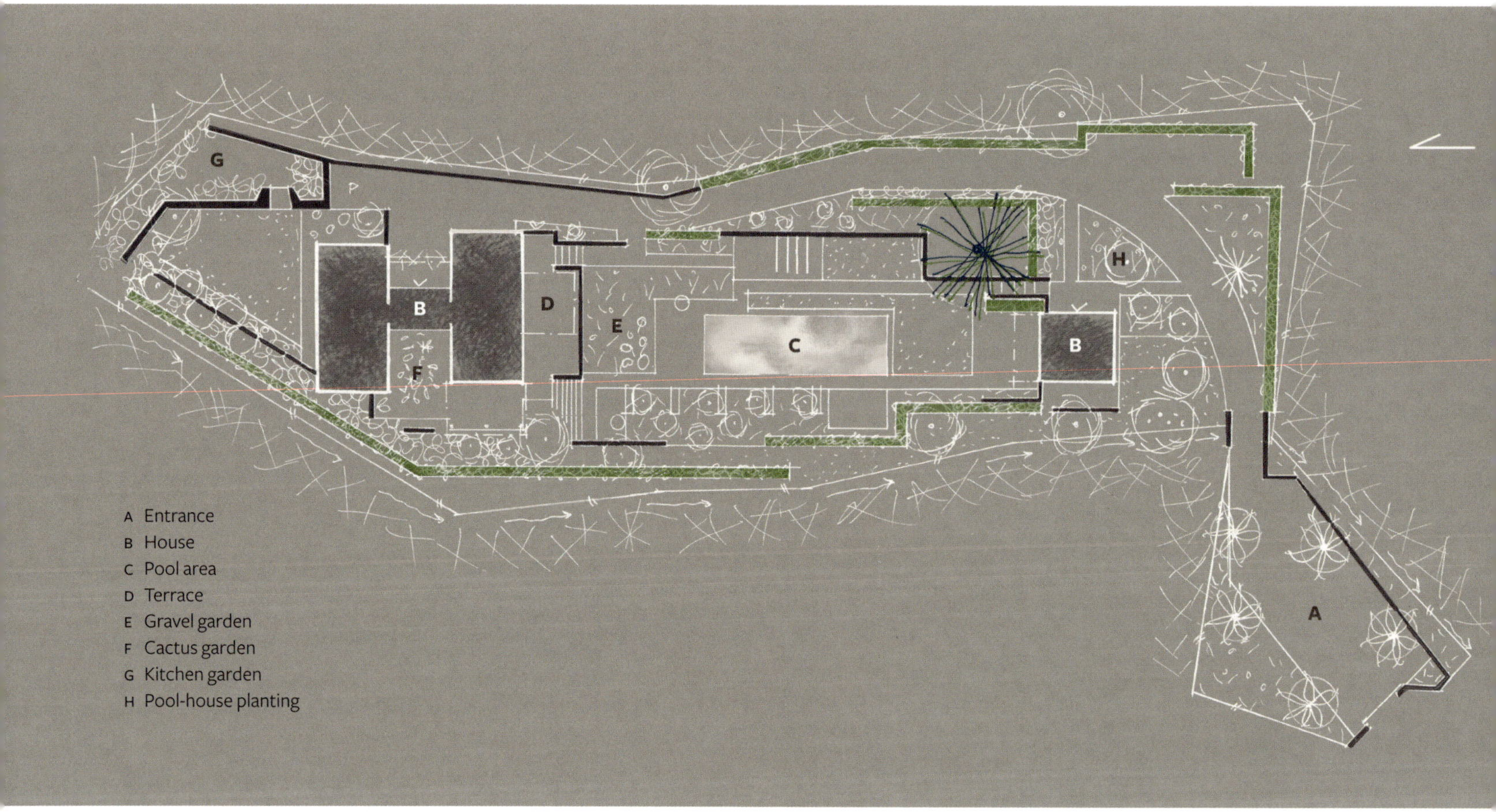

White roses in both bush and standard forms are underplanted with Mexican fleabane and Russian sage, against a backdrop of walls and hedges the same height. The ceramic bull by Ulla and Gustav Kraitz grazes in a meadow of Chinese fountain grass.

The surroundings

The adventure continued when my friends Lisen Stibeck and John Larsson, who had started building a house in St-Tropez, visited the Chelsea Flower Show and fell in love with my Laurent-Perrier garden. This led to a commission to create a garden for them in the South of France. It was at the exhibition in London that the idea was born to apply some of the design elements of my garden to their new home, and also to reuse parts of things that had been made specially for the exhibition garden.

La Moutte is the name of the place where this was all going to happen. There was once an olive grove there, the traces of which tell the story of the farm. In this gently undulating landscape, old pine trees hide the villas and colour the hills green. The height, design and colour of the houses are strictly and consciously regulated, to reinforce the impression of farmland. This was to be the site of the new house and pool house, with a garden tucked into a south-facing slope with a large terrace that rises above the garden and looks out across the surroundings. In this already delightful setting, I was to create a garden.

A scented entrance

What could be better than entering a scented enclosure? In Sweden we associate this in particular with old gardens with blackcurrant bushes or rambling roses at their entrances.

Wild mimosa was growing by the entrance to the garden in St-Tropez, providing flowers and delicious scent as early as February. The mimosa shows the way to the gate, which leads to an enclosed space surrounded by fencing. This area creates excitement and anticipation, but is also somewhere to stop and be welcomed before you go further. I chose to cover the fencing with two scented roses: 'Pierre de Ronsard', with full, cupped flowers, and the contrasting 'Sweet Love' with its elegant pink flowers. The roses flower successively and spread their fragrance throughout the season. This space was once used for parking, and it needed greenery to create a feeling of intimacy. Now a group of tall date palms (*Phoenix dactilifera*) and Japanese silver grass (*Miscanthus sinensis* 'Emmanuel Lepage') provide character and volume. This area is separated from the garden and its new, low-key Provençal-style buildings.

BELOW In front of a striking ceramic pumpkin by Hans Hedberg, Chinese fountain grass and irises catch the light.

OPPOSITE A mask by Hertha Hillfon rests among succulents in front of a wall of local stone.

Anticipation

The entrance leads first to a small pool house, the door to which faces a fragrant area of flowers beneath an old olive tree. This gives a rural impression, and the small terrace in front of the building makes the scale intimate. The area is underplanted with red and blue sage (*Salvia microphylla* 'Bordeaux' and 'Royal Blue'), interspersed with giant feather grass (*Stipa gigantea*) with its rust-brown seed heads, red-hot pokers (*Kniphofia praecox*) in shades of red-brown, lavender-blue Russian sage (*Perovskia* 'Little Spire') and rust-brown stonecrop (*Hylotelephium* 'Herbstfreude'). Clipped cushions of Delavay privet (*Ligustrum delavayanum*) and Japanese holly (*Ilex crenata* 'Stokes') provide structure all year round.

A bird-of-paradise tree (*Erythrostemon gilliesii*), a native of Australia, enhances the light character of the planting in this area. When it is in bloom, the yellow and warm orange butterfly-like flowers give a romantic feel to the red-plastered pool house, making it a favourite plant in the sunny landscape.

The idea for the entire garden is based on visually inviting in the surrounding landscape – in the same way that Vésian did to enhance perspective and create a feeling of space – while at the same time creating a tight framework. I did this with stone walls and various types of hedging that follow the way the buildings interact with the landscape. The garden thus appears to be a cohesive whole, its differences in level reinforced by steps, walls and planting.

The drive leads through hedges and walls to the main entrance, set in a fully glazed corridor between the two buildings that make up the main house. The entrance area has been paved with cobbles beneath a pergola covered with white-flowered *Wisteria sinensis* 'Alba', which provides light shade.

On the other side of the glazed passageway I created a succulent garden centred on a large sculpted face by the ceramicist Hertha Hillfon. This tells us that the family who live here have a great love for and understanding of art. The artwork and succulents are united by a powerful shared design language: the candelabra aloe (*Aloe arborescens*), in particular, brings the space alive with its impressive rust-red flower spikes that reflect the colour of the terracotta.

The succulent garden is characterized by vigorous groups of candelabra aloe, stemmed hedgehog agave (*Agave stricta*) and soft-leaved fox agave (*A. attenuata*) planted against a background of dwarf pomegranate (*Punica granatum* 'Nana') and white-flowered coastal rosemary (*Westringia fruticosa* 'Alba'). A wall of local stone in front of tall cypress hedges closes off the small garden room and, together with the tall-stemmed agaves, brings visual depth to this garden, a kind of display cabinet seen from the entrance.

Clipped spheres of Delavay privet bring structure to relaxed planting.

Form and colour

One of the requirements of this project was to integrate the family's sculpture collection into the garden. This was a fantastic task and a great source of inspiration for me. Art has always been part of gardening culture, and it is particularly rewarding when it is included from the outset. The transparent architecture of the house means that the art both inside and out is tied together in a dialogue that enhances the experience of being there.

The family spend a lot of time in the seating area outside the kitchen and dining room, preferably with a book in hand. This is really what everyone wants their garden to be: a welcoming hideaway in which to enjoy spending time. I am always delighted to see just how well used this raised terrace is.

Below the terrace I created a gravel garden with sculptures by Hans Hedberg set among the plants. The natural shapes of the egg, plum, lemon and pumpkin are incredibly beautiful, with their crystalline glazes in the vivid colours that were Hedberg's trademark. The height of the giant feather grass adds lightness as it catches the sun and is swayed by the breeze, while balls of Delavay privet lend weight and depth to the planting.

To complement the warm-hued gravel surface, I chose austere plants in a grey-green palette. They include sandpaper sotol (*Dasylirion serratifolium*) and the pride of Madeira (*Echium candicans*), with its metre-high blue flower spikes that come into bloom in April and June, at the same time as the Mediterranean spurge (*Euphorbia characias* subsp. 'Wulfenii') produces its lime-yellow bracts.

Early-flowering perennials planted in groups provide an intense spring season that transforms the gravel garden into a sea of colour, like a watercolour painting. The display consists of irises in shades of pale blue and black (*Iris* Germanica group 'Jane Phillips' and 'Black Swan'), among other irises, lemon-white red-hot pokers (*Kniphofia* 'Ice Queen'), yellow kangaroo paw (*Anigozanthos flavidus*) and blue-black *Agapanthus* 'Black Pantha'. Carpets of Mexican fleabane (*Erigeron karvinskianus*), canary clover (*Lotus hirsutus* 'Fréjorques') and grey stonecrop (*Rhodiola pachyclados*) contribute to a palette with accents of pale blue and blue-black. Additional apricot and pinkish-white elements embed and emphasize Hedberg's organic forms. The colours flow together and the transitory nature of the flowers in the gravel garden is a recurring theme. When the short spring season is over, the plants retain their shape and structure, with repeated groups of Mexican fleabane, *Gaura lindheimeri* and the tall stems of feather grass.

Small areas of lawn around the pool provide a restful open space framed by hedges and walls. Here, a natural feeling has been created with the help of the soft Chinese fountain grass (*Pennisetum alopecuroides* 'Hameln'), from which white oleander trees (*Nerium oleander* 'Mont Blanc') rise and flower almost all summer long. Set into the grass are rectangular blocks of yew (*Taxus baccata*) cut into sloping shapes, reused from my 2013 Chelsea show garden. The grasses are also interspersed with late-flowering perennials, such as coneflower (*Echinacea*) and giant verbena (*Verbena bonariensis*), which prolong the flowering season. An oxblood-red bull made by the Swedish ceramicists Ulla and Gustav Kraitz grazes in a patch of fountain grass.

The rustic pergola, with its afternoon shade, has become the focal point. Strong oak beams rest on a stone wall that supports a copper roof.

Boundaries

On the Riviera, wild boar and heavy downpours have led to many gardens being surrounded by deep ditches and strong fences. This is the case at Villa La Moutte, and to conceal

Steps of local granite lead to a small kitchen garden containing herbs, including rosemary, thyme and various forms of sage, planted among rocks. The prolific Mexican fleabane scrambles over and around them.

them, I used tall hedges and climbing plants. The framing consists of different types of hedging for variety and to link the garden to its surroundings. The choice of species also takes into account the differing conditions of the various areas of the garden.

Along the drive, in the shade of woodland beyond the boundary of the property, I planted a hedge of cherry laurel (*Prunus laurocerasus* 'Novita') that is kept lightly trimmed. With its shiny, dark green leaves, it reinforces and marks the edge of the woodland. The drive is separated from the garden by double hedges: first a low line of Yeddo hawthorn (*Rhaphiolepis umbellata* 'Ovata'), with its defined, leathery leaves and pinkish-white flowers, then a taller hedge of pineapple guava (*Feijoa sellowiania*). Both are extremely tolerant of drought. The garden is bordered to the west by a classic tall cypress hedge (*Cupressus* × *leylandii*), and to the north by free-growing mastic trees (*Pistacia lentiscus*), which grow wild around the Mediterranean.

The seasons

The South of France is at its loveliest in the spring, when the wildlife and gardens come to life, increasingly often after a wet winter. When the mimosa flowers in February, it is the equivalent of carpets of wood anemones in

Red baby sage (*Salvia microphylla* 'Bordeaux') and Russian sage in the foreground. In the background is clipped coastal rosemary (*Westringia fruticosa*) with Mexican sage (*S. leucantha*), which sends up spikes of blue flowers in late summer.

northern Europe: the blossom is intense and the air filled with the characteristic scent. In April wisteria covers all the pergolas, closely followed in May and June by roses and bougainvillea. For me, this is the essence of spring and early summer in this part of the world.

The problems of climate change

In all Mediterranean gardens, it is primarily trees and shrubs that produce the flowers, and in recent years I have noticed how high temperatures as early as May are making everything flower earlier than before. The agapanthus are already out in the middle of June, and from then on it is the architecture of the garden – the trees, bushes and hedges – that gives the season its character. The warm summer evenings associated with the Mediterranean are also coming earlier in the year, and the heat causes stress in plants, often causing them to drop their leaves.

In this region climate change is keenly felt. It is often windy, and the heavy rains that used to usher in the autumn are now spread over the whole year. These days it is possible to plant successfully only in the cooler half of the year, because the rest of the year is too hot.

Many of the pests that are thriving in the changing climate have given me a very stark awakening. It is especially painful to observe their ravages when a great deal of effort has been put into providing good soil for plants that have been ambitiously yet carefully chosen. After just one year, for example, we could see that the lavender beds were failing – and that happened very quickly. In this case the culprit turned out to be a bacterium called *Xylella fastidiosa*, which also attacks rosemary, olive trees, laurel, oleander, gorse and euphorbia, among many other plants. Once it is present, there's nothing you can do except replace the affected plants with species that are not susceptible.

Just as in Sweden, various forms of mildew are rampant in the Mediterranean. Now, at last, in this time of climate fluctuation, the nurseries on the Riviera are making great progress with sourcing a variety of sustainable plants, many of them local. For instance, more resistant species of lavender are being introduced from North Africa. In this garden, however, I chose to replace the infested lavender with shaped coastal rosemary, which produces small blue flowers, and the taller Mexican bush sage (*Salvia leucantha*).

Beetles of various types are also found here in large numbers, including bark beetles, which attack pines and laurel. Even lawns can be badly affected by cutworms (the larvae of *Agrostis ipsilon*), and are treated with nematodes. Aphids of various types are combated with ladybirds, the two-spot *Adalia bipunctata*.

To encourage the many useful insects that also exist, this garden contains many plants that are valuable and attractive to them, for instance various forms of salvia.

The garden of tomorrow

I always try to make planting plans based on the conditions of the site. Over the years I have sought out good, ecologically mindful nurseries that offer an increasingly wide assortment of plants adapted to the warming climate. Many of these are based in Australia and North Africa, where the climate is extreme.

The soil on the Riviera is generally heavy and water-retentive, and must therefore be supplemented with grit, pumice and organic material. The timing of planting is also of great importance. Trees that are put in after March have trouble establishing, no matter how high the quality. We experienced this during our work at La Moutte. After a few replacements, the trees are now doing well, even if they are still the target of all manner of pest.

Another major challenge is effective drainage to remove excess water quickly in the event of torrential rain, which would otherwise remain standing in the garden and cause significant damage to the growing plants. The trees – and indeed the rest of the plants – in the garden contribute to this and to a favourable microclimate. Through the use of more drought-tolerant local plants, the need for artificial irrigation is also reduced, thus helping to prevent harmful fungal diseases.

A garden is a living organism that requires both knowledge and love over time, no matter where it is located. It is naive to imagine that a garden on the Riviera is easier to care for simply because the climate is warmer. I would actually say that it requires greater effort than a garden in northern Europe, increasingly linked to the climate fluctuation that is a fact of life today.

The flowers of the bird-of-paradise tree, which is also seen in the centre of the photograph opposite.

OVERLEAF Morning light illuminates the clipped and free-growing parts of the garden, and creates contrasts in form and colour. On the path to the right of the pool is a sculpture by the Danish artist Robert Jacobsen. The sloping yew hedges stand in a carpet of moor grass (*Sesleria nitida*), and between the hedges are high-crowned white-flowered oleander trees. On the left is a shade-giving loggia of blackened oak with a suspended copper roof resting on a wall of local stone. The old pine tree – the garden's protector – also contributes to the shadiness of this area.

Villa Lumen

A Mediterranean dream from the 1930s, given new life

A dormant, overgrown villa garden with a view of the Mediterranean is given a longed-for restoration with a focus on beauty and biodiversity.

My first meeting with Paul and Stephanie couldn't have been better: a weekday dinner around the kitchen table surrounded by children playing. Paul wanted to pass on aspects of his own childhood in Provence – with sun-ripened tomatoes, aubergines and perfumed roses – to his own family. The couple sought a house with antique charm that was close to the sea, and after a long search they found this one on the Cap d'Antibes. It is a house with a story to tell, in a landscape with century-old pine trees that had seen this summer residence grow up on the headland.

Dreams

The house was in good condition, beautifully proportioned and with many exquisite details. A large terrace and well-positioned pool were beautifully nestled in greenery, while the rest of the garden had sadly been abandoned, the driveway covered in concrete. During that unforgettable evening, my gut feeling was that the task would be complex, but Paul and Stephanie's genuineness, interest and thoughtfulness prompted a desire to reawaken the slumbering garden for the growing family, to preserve and simultaneously develop it.

What did Paul and Stephanie's dreams look like? There were many individual ambitions, such as removing the concrete to make room for greenery, and creating structure and places where you wanted to linger and explore the garden's plants. It was a true joy to create the first design sketches for such engaged clients.

The site

The 1930s villa enjoys the shade cast by a canopy of pine trees. The view is magical, and the cicadas provide the same soundtrack now as they did a hundred years ago, when the coast of this peninsula became so popular – along with the many plant nurseries that were on the headland at the time. At the end of the nineteenth century the peninsula was dominated by olive trees, vineyards and vegetable farms. An old postcard reveals that a century ago anemones were grown

The Riviera in March, with early flowers: mauve wallflowers (*Erysimum* 'Bowles's Mauve') with rust-red tree aloe (*Aloe aborescens*). There are large clumps of sandpaper sotol (*Dasylirion serratifolium*), orange-yellow *Bulbine latifolia* syn. *transvaalensis* and Mexican feather grass (*Stipa tenuissima*), with white society garlic (*Tulbaghia violacea* 'Alba') in the foreground.

The new flight of steps.

here commercially, followed in the 1930s by carnations. But gradually, rose-growing became more common, only to disappear more or less in the 1980s. The remains of the nurseries can be seen to this day.

It's my first visit, and I wait outside the main gate, full of anticipation. When it opens, I am overwhelmed by the period villa set high above the garden, and the rocky setting with a view of the Mediterranean. The location, house and view are dreamlike and magical, like something out of an old Hollywood movie.

The fairytale setting around the slumbering villa, with its closed shutters and classical terraces, takes my breath away before I start to take in the reality. I am standing in front of a neglected jewel, hidden beneath a blanket of ageing trees, climbing plants and tangled undergrowth. Strange concrete structures and overgrown beds speak of the decay of the past century. Ancient trees of great character, such as olives (*Olea europaea*), cork oaks (*Quercus suber*) and American pepper (*Schinus molle*), give a strong feeling of the Mediterranean, behind stone walls covered with star jasmine (*Trachelospermum jasminoides*). I am captivated by the setting, but it is the large cushions of rosemary (*Rosmarinus officinalis*) hanging over the rocks, and the high-crowned myrtles and oleanders, that floor me.

I was not quite so excited when I stepped into the garden on the north side of the villa, which was completely overgrown. But there were valuable trees even here, including another American pepper and a mastic tree (*Pistacia lentiscus*), which could be saved and highlighted in the redesign of the garden.

The process

The first thing I did was survey the terrain, with its rocks, walls, steps, trees and shrubs. It was clear that the next task would be to remove the concrete, laid in the 1960s, which divided the garden and reduced it visually. The aim of my design was to refine and develop the site by creating clearly discernible spaces and qualities, as well as by introducing flowering elements to reinject life into the garden.

My French contractor, Franck, with whom I had previously worked on a garden in St-Tropez, was involved from the outset. This was fortunate, not only because of his experience and contacts, but also because of the rewarding dialogue that took place throughout the process. His ambition stretched so far that he started to learn English, and pretty soon his colleagues joined in too, while I have to confess to never really progressing beyond my schoolboy French. But with regular meetings on site and by sharing digital images, we were on our way.

The concrete surfaces and walls would be demolished, and half-dead bushes and trees removed. Tree surgeons began by inspecting the crowns of the trees I had chosen to save. Once the garden had been cleared, it was easier to see what could be done; my visits to the site also allowed me to understand what it was possible to achieve, which is essential when working on a garden that already exists. The rejuvenated trees recovered quickly and were already putting on new growth before we had really got going with the new garden.

My goal was to create harmony between the various garden rooms, to open up and connect them with steps and paths where necessary. The intention was to give the different parts their own character and content by making use of the prevailing light conditions in each. In this way, the rear garden was tailored to become a shady garden in tones of green – a truly exciting prospect.

The entrance

The main entrance of the villa is approached via a classical flight of steps that has, since the 1960s, been framed by tall cypresses and trimmed myrtle in an expanse of white agapanthus and dark red bougainvillea. These plants, which more than any others symbolize the dream of a Mediterranean garden, were a good foundation on which to build once the garage and surrounding concrete area had been converted into a gym and garden. We removed the large expanses of concrete and the overgrown climbers on the walls, and saved the white agapanthus for reuse. There was already a clear concept, but it needed upgrading to fit in with the lower part of the garden.

I connected the different parts of the garden with shallow steps. Using natural local stone, I introduced walls in the form of large, vertical stone blocks, and an old, neglected pattern of intricate paving in the grass was uncovered to create a sense of wholeness, identity and welcome without the need for continuous paving – a simple way to make the garden feel bigger. New stone edging was installed in the beds before the agapanthus was replanted within a border of low-growing African box (*Myrsine africana*). This very drought-tolerant species replaced a damaged box hedge (*Buxus*

Reconstructed paving is interplanted with grass. Old shrubs have been cut into softer shapes, such as the myrtle (*Myrtus communis*) closest to the wall. In the foreground are grey-leaved tree germander (*Teucrium fruticans*) and Australian laurel (*Pittosporum tobira* 'Nanum'). On the middle terrace groups of New Zealand flax (*Phormium tenax*) grow beneath the old holm oak (*Quercus ilex*).

LEFT The first thing you encounter when you enter the garden is a mosaic of flagstones and grass, framed by large beds of white agapanthus behind low hedges of African box. Pruned white oleander trees (*Nerium oleander* 'Mont Blanc') mark the entrance to the lower garden. In the background is an American pepper tree with its pendulous branches.

ABOVE The elegant sculpture *Celine* in patinated bronze by Paul's father, Jim Ritchie, is seen against a wall that is almost entirely covered with creeping fig.

BELOW Replanted blue and white agapanthus and hydrangeas in the gentle shade of an olive tree.

OPPOSITE Newly built steps connect the terraces and offer a magnificent view of the Mediterranean.

sempervirens) – an increasingly rare sight on the Riviera.

Creeping fig (*Ficus pumila*) was planted around the garage, and now, after just a few years, it covers most of the walls. The idea is to create a volume of green and an effective background for a bronze sculpture, *Celine*, which welcomes visitors to the garden and was made by Paul's father, the internationally renowned sculptor Jim Ritchie (1929–2017). From there, steps lead up to the main entrance and the upper terrace, with its swimming pool, surrounded by olive trees and lavender. Overlooking the Mediterranean Sea, it is a terrace for outdoor living in all seasons.

The steps and rock face

When a rock face in front of the house was exposed, it was found to be in very poor condition. We improvised a solution with large stone blocks to strengthen it and to provide support for a grand flight of steps that was planned to lead down to the garden. Once the work was finished, a new structure emerged with a south-facing planting area, and the pruned rosemary bushes regained their starring role. These steps became the background motif for the whole garden. With a comfortably low tread height, they make their way between rocks and the salvaged pine trees that enhance the perspective and give the garden depth.

The lower terrace

The next step was to open up the lower garden. Around a mature American pepper tree, a large grass area was needed for play and exercise. We started by moving some large shrubs and an old olive tree out towards the boundary of the plot. Even old olives are relatively easy to move, because they have a consolidated root system. By reusing existing shrubs, such as myrtle, abelia and oleander, in new positions, we were able to make use of their size and shapes.

The large pepper tree, with its characteristic drooping branches that brush the lawn, underwent successive prunings to rejuvenate it as much as possible. In the partial shade behind it, we established a large bed with a wide border of reused agapanthus. Groups of blue *Hydrangea macrophylla* 'Blaumeise' interspersed with specimen shrubs, such as winter-flowering white *Camellia japonica* 'Snowball' and Japanese andromeda (*Pieris japonica*), with low cherry laurel hedges (*Prunus laurocerasus* 'Mount

Vernon') and, among other things, spring-flowering Chinese dogwood (*Cornus kousa* var. *chinensis*), give the bed character in the spring and summer.

Closer to the entrance, where the light penetrates beneath the olive tree, we established a bed containing pruned shrubs, including Delavay privet (*Ligustrum delavayanum*), coastal rosemary (*Westringia fruticosa* 'Alba') and dwarf pomegranate (*Punica granatum* 'Nana'). Here, solitary shrubs have been pruned into an open form, to give an airier impression; these include the chaste tree (*Vitex agnus-castus*), the dark-leaved Texas mountain laurel (*Sophora secundiflora*) and the bird-of-paradise tree (*Erythrostemon gilliesii*), the yellow-orange butterfly-like flowers of which rise up from the bed.

The walls of the garden are covered with star jasmine and lemon-scented Azorean jasmine (*Jasminum azoricum*). These evergreen climbers covered the walls and fences in just two seasons, creating an effective backdrop to the garden.

The shade garden

Behind the house, the conditions were right for a new garden room, shaded by the villa in the middle of the day. A few existing trees and plants – an American pepper tree, a large mastic bush and a tall bamboo hedge on the boundary of the plot – formed a good framework for this new shade garden. To my mind, the word bamboo conjures up moisture, sparkling light and the sound of leaves rustling in the breeze. Here the shade was the great asset in a place where the heat can often feel oppressive. The intention was to create a separate room with a dining area and comfortable furniture to relax on.

Creating a shade garden in such favourable conditions was a dream come true for me. After correcting the significant differences in level by building a wall, I was able to create a larger terrace on two levels. The root system of the existing trees also influenced the design, and a low protective wall was built around the mastic tree. At the same time, the idea of using a tall, decorative wall as a backdrop for the tree was born. For me, the embodiment of light and shade is central: it brings the garden to life. The use of elegant vegetation in front of a wall creates both depth and a background motif.

Around that time I attended a presentation about the celebrated architect Le Corbusier's use of colours made from natural pigments. It took place against an Yves Klein-blue wall, and at that moment the wall in the garden became that colour. The shade garden would be based on leaf structures in shades of green and red, with a few select flowers in white and blue.

After visiting Paul's father's home, it became obvious that we had also created the ideal setting for his sensual sculpture *Family* (1966). We placed it in front of the blue wall, surrounded by a carpet of dark-leaved, white-flowered lilyturf (*Liriope* 'Monroe White'). Against the wall we planted red-leaved *Alocasia macrorrhiza* 'Blue Heaven', with blue spiderwort (*Tradescantia* 'Zwanenburg Blue') beneath. The large leaves of the alocasia, in combination with a rough tree fern (*Cyathea australis*) that catches the light, give the arrangement a delicate airiness that is stunning when seen against the backdrop of the blue wall.

I love building up garden rooms scenographically. In the shade garden there was bamboo on the boundary, with the neighbour's mature trees as a backdrop, so I chose to add red-leaved banana, red-leaved cabbage palm (*Cordyline australis* 'Purpurea') and winter-flowering *Mahonia × media* 'Charity', along with various forms of tree fern. These offer a delicacy and beauty that are hard to beat. I used the soft tree fern (*Dicksonia antarctica*) and the narrow-stemmed rough tree fern as feature plants for the entire shade garden. The tropical feeling is enhanced by a group of palm court palms

OPPOSITE The new fern garden around the old mastic tree. In the background are shady palms and tree ferns of various types. In the foreground is *Mandevilla* 'White'.

ABOVE Fern leaves are mirrored against the Yves Klein-blue wall, underplanted with deep blue spiderwort.

OVERLEAF The wonderful foliage of the rough tree fern, underplanted with dark-leaved, white-flowered lilyturf.

PAGE 217 Soft tree ferns are seen against a background of red-leaved cabbage palm and bamboo, underplanted with Japanese forest grass and ferns.

The bronze sculpture *Family* by Jim Ritchie sits in a bed of lilyturf in front of the blue wall. The planting around the beautiful mastic tree is of red-leaved alocasia and dark-blue spiderwort, with the magnificent foliage of the red-leaved banana and tree ferns.

PRACTICAL PLANTS

The increasingly hot summers of this area mean that it has become more difficult to grow fruit trees. I have therefore chosen relatively heat-resistant varieties, such as almond (*Prunus dulcis*) and various kinds of citrus, including lemon (*Citrus × limon* 'Eureka') and fingered citron (*C. medica* var. *sarcodactylis*). Fruit bushes, including thornless blackberries (*Rubus laciniatus* 'Thornless Evergreen') and tayberries (*R.* 'Tayberry'), grow against one wall in a lightly shaded part of the garden. There is also space for lettuce, tomatoes and strawberries – to the great delight of the resident squirrels. Only small quantities are grown here, but they are of different varieties for a long harvesting period.

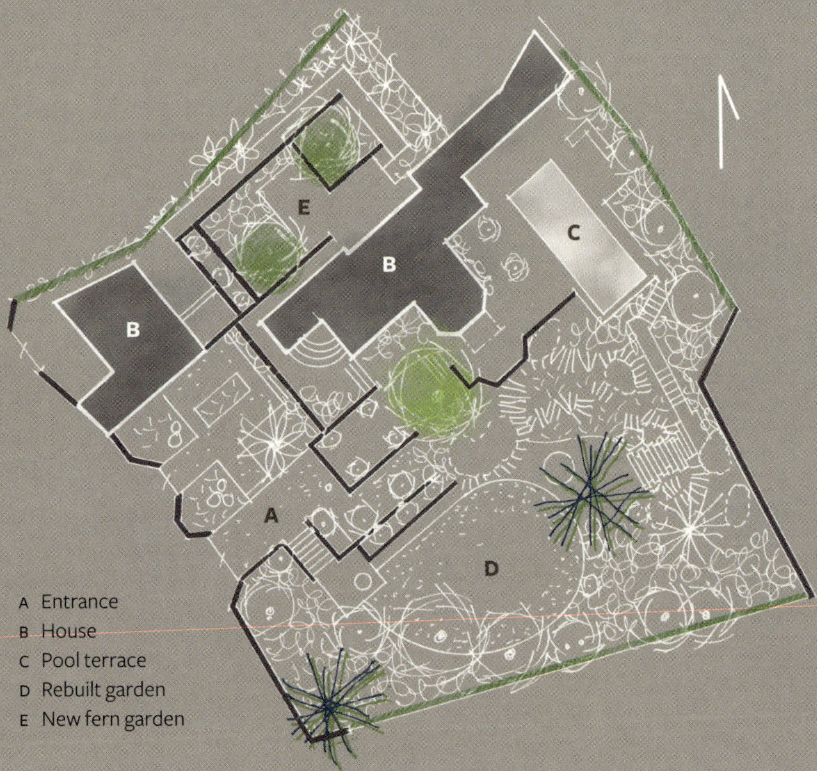

A Entrance
B House
C Pool terrace
D Rebuilt garden
E New fern garden

1 Agapanthus (*Agapanthus africanus*)
2 Mexican fleabane (*Erigeron karvinskianus*)
3 Smooth hydrangea (*Hydrangea arborescens* 'Annabelle')
4 Rough tree fern (*Cyathea australis*)
5 Japanese forest grass (*Hakonechloa macra*)
6 Spiderwort (*Tradescantia* 'Zwanenburg Blue')
7 Salvia (*Salvia chamaedryoides × macrophylla*)
8 New tree-fern leaves
9 Society garlic (*Tulbaghia violacea* 'Alba')

(*Howea forsteriana*) and bamboo palms (*Rhapis excelsa*) with a backdrop of climbing hydrangea (*Hydrangea petiolaris*) to hide the surrounding fence. The palms also create shade, a necessity for the establishment and survival of the tree ferns while we wait for the reduced tree crowns to spread after dead and damaged branches were removed.

Low underplanting with various types of lilyturf and fern emphasizes the striking stems of the palms and tree ferns. The lushness of the vegetation in shades of green and purple, with varying leaf structures, helps to embed the terrace in its setting and provides great variety in the different light conditions that prevail over the course of the day. This is truly a place of peace and quiet.

Plant choice and climate

Even in classic Mediterranean gardens, climate fluctuation is posing new challenges. Specialized nurseries offer an ever-increasing range of organic shrubs native to Africa, Mexico and Australia, while perennials are rare because of the hot summers. For instance, it is becoming more common to use Delavay privet instead of box, and, for low edging, hybrid germander (*Teucrium × lucidrys*) is an excellent alternative. Similarly, dark blue *Salvia chamaedryoides × macrophylla* and Russian sage (*Perovskia* 'Filigran') are good African substitutes for native lavender (*Lavandula angustifolia*). African blue lavender (*L.* × *allardii* 'African Pride') is another alternative to the more common varieties, which are prone to attack by the bacterium *Xylella fastidiosa*. The Mexican native giant hesperaloe (*Hesperaloe funifera*), a red-flowered relative of agave; the bird-of-paradise tree, with its orange-yellow butterfly-like flowers; and the blue-flowered glory bush (*Tibouchina urvilleana*) – the last two both from Australia – are other new acquaintances in the wake of climate change.

A maturing dream

Now that the garden has had a few years to grow and develop, it is clear to see how it embraces and enhances the relationship between the villa and its surroundings. There is now a greater variety of flowering plants that highlight the passing of the different seasons. Even during the garden's winter hibernation, the bright red buds of tree aloe shimmer, and the 2-metre-tall spikes of pride of Madeira (*Echium candicans*) reach for the skies early in the year. The purple-blue cushions of wallflowers also announce the arrival of spring, closely followed by hydrangeas and the first scented flowers of the citrus trees. Wisteria, star jasmine and rosemary all flower in April, and the roses and bird-of-paradise trees in May – to mention just a few examples.

During the month of June, lavender and sage, the white oleander trees and agapanthus all start to flower, marking the high point in the flowering season. From then on, it is greenery and structure that give the garden character and variety. Bushes are trimmed several times during the growing season, which never really stops. It is the abundant evergreen vegetation, which in winter forms such a powerful contrast to the shrubs that lose their leaves, that makes the Mediterranean garden so interesting.

With the knowledge of organic soil and well-adapted plant material produced to as great an extent as possible by local nurseries, together with a highly motivated team who have demonstrated great knowledge and patience during both installation and maintenance, I have found a wonderful way to create a garden. In a short time it has developed to enhance the original character of the site.

The climate change we can already observe, which brings early summer heat, heavy rain and a great deal of wind, affects plants in various unpredictable ways. The dream of the

Mediterranean garden, therefore – in all its beauty – now demands more knowledge and experience than ever before. I had the privilege of being able to follow this project from start to finish. It remains a garden whose development I follow with great interest, and to which I long to return.

OPPOSITE The old garage was converted into a gym and equipped with lighting that emphasizes the green facade and the flagstones set into the grass.

ABOVE Shallow steps of local granite lead up to the path through the ferns. The foliage and fern stems are emphasized by the lighting. Rough tree fern is in the foreground.

The illuminated steps and pine tree tie the garden together both physically and visually. The sandpit and granite bench make this area a destination in the garden.

LIGHTING

The lighting in the garden serves several purposes: it gives a welcoming feeling when you enter through the gate; it creates security and beauty in the garden; and, above all, it provides beautiful views from inside the villa in the evening. It highlights the garden's different rooms and their characters, as well as sight lines and individual objects.

We use fixtures with different light properties, with warm-toned and white light as the base. By using different strengths and varying the distribution, priority can be given to what needs to be emphasized. Soft light on the wall gives a sense of space, while the light on the pine tree highlights it as an object. The lighting also emphasizes the different scales of the garden, from the downward lighting at the entrance to the uplighting that makes the pine tree look monumental in the evening.

Such variation creates anticipation in the observer. The restrained nature of the fittings is a conscious choice, to let the light itself rather than the fittings be the important thing. Objects are highlighted in different ways. A dark sculpture gets an illuminated background, the blue wall crisp light and the broad flight of steps low bollards to illuminate the steps and surrounding plants. Using light, we conjure up the character of the garden in the evening, when light is just as important as darkness.

Torbjörn Eliasson, lighting architect

Change

Climate, hardiness and biodiversity

In a time of climate change, we must adapt to new conditions, not least in our choice of plants. And, as biodiversity decreases in farmland and forestry, the importance of making a contribution in parks and gardens is increasing.

This chapter is devoted to my experiences in Sweden; the consequences of climate change in southern Europe are addressed in the relevant garden chapters.

Climate

In the north of Sweden, the length of the growing season has increased by approximately two weeks in the past forty years alone. It has also increased in the south of Sweden, albeit by less, and there the increase has occurred largely since about 2010.

Of course, this might sound like a good thing from the perspective of agriculture, forestry and horticulture. However, it also increases the risk of attack by new pests, insects and fungi, and of invasive species spreading at the expense of native flora.

One negative effect of climate change that is already apparent is increased temperature fluctuation in late winter. Early periods of warmth prompt plants to start their spring growth prematurely. If this is followed by one or more periods of frost, it can cause significant damage to the plants – a consequence that can also affect birds and insects through lack of food. A warmer climate and more wind also mean that plants require more water, which in periods of low rainfall can cause stress that results in pest attack and drought damage.

The depth of snow cover varies greatly from year to year in Sweden, and this has led to more ice forming in the north of the country. Climate change means that the average rainfall will increase significantly, particularly in the winter. It can also lead to extreme downpours, as well as summer droughts and forest fires. Extreme weather events (heat, precipitation, drought, floods) are becoming more common in our changing climate, and they have a major impact on plants.

Hardiness

Sweden, which is nearly 1,600 km from north to south, naturally has great differences in climate from one region to another, and this has always affected our choice of plants. Since the 1980s the Swedish University of Agricultural Sciences (SLU) has selected a variety of trees and shrubs to broaden and secure the range available for both public environments and private gardens. These have been tested for their ability to withstand climate change and to resist pests and diseases, as well as for their structure, flowers, fruit and autumn colour, and they are divided according to the country's climate zones. The result is a relatively broad range of plants that have been given a designation of quality, the 'E-mark'. The number of E-marked varieties is limited, and today consists of about 160 trees and shrubs, as well as about 90 fruit trees and berry-bearing plants.

In countries with harsh winters, choosing plants based on their geographical habitat, or provenance, is vital for their survival. Their growth rhythm is crucial: when they start growing, and when they stop in the autumn and go into dormancy. In large parts of Sweden, the E-mark system with its associated zone designations is a prerequisite for being able to design and plan parks and gardens containing a range of plants. Research and selection work is conducted by the SLU and the nursery industry to develop the range of shrubs and trees adapted to the changing climate, and to offer a broader variety of plants. For me, the E-mark system has been crucial to my ability to design and plan parks and gardens with greater botanical diversity in the northernmost parts of the country. The same knowledge can be applied to other areas of the northern hemisphere with a similar continental climate.

Perennials, on the other hand, cannot be divided into climate zones, because the drainage, snow cover and microclimate of each location are crucially important to whether they survive every winter or reach maturity – both prerequisites for being considered hardy. Within the same garden environment there are generally several different microclimates. These can be enhanced and – as I demonstrate through examples in this book – designed to create protective planting areas and the most favourable growing conditions possible.

Gently sloping beds in which water is never left standing are the best way to avoid winter damage in all gardens. This is a simple piece of advice, as useful in the north as it is in the south.

Plants for northern climates up to 63° north

The midnight light in the north of Sweden is of great importance to the rapid growth of vegetation at the start of the growing season. In the plant lists on pages 232–4, I have divided some of the absolute best bulbs and perennials for 63° north into those that flower in the spring, summer and late summer. The selected perennials stay healthy, are relatively long-lived and have a long flowering period thanks to the combination of cool, bright summer nights and warm, sunny days. I have refrained from including perennials that don't have time to flower before autumn puts an end to the season.

Smaller trees and shrubs are also presented here on the basis of climate adaptation, character, flowers, scent and autumn colour. The selection reflects the longer growing season that is one result of climate change, and these are plants of which I have more than forty years of accumulated experience. They work just as well in the north of Sweden as in the rest of the country and other parts of northern Europe.

For southern and central Sweden up to 63° north, I focus on late-flowering perennials and grasses – species that do not have time to bloom in the north. I have not included bulbs because the range is limitless once you move further south. Within the selection of trees and shrubs, I have focused on varieties that flower in the winter and early spring – something that isn't possible further north than 63°.

Biodiversity

In a landscape of increasingly industrialized agriculture and forestry, horticultural environments are becoming more and more important. Through the wide variety of shelter and food they offer to both birds and insects, they are valuable areas of diversity. In other words, gardens and parks have become an increasingly important complement to the nature that we as humans are rapidly changing.

Fergus Garrett, head gardener of the renowned Great Dixter in East Sussex, southern England, has studied the botanical diversity of that garden in comparison with the surrounding meadows and woodland. The results show that the variety and richness of species in the garden are far greater than in the landscape around it. Richness of species and valuable habitats in our gardens and parks are an important resource for countering the reduction of biodiversity in densely populated areas. There is also a lot of unused potential here, since too many gardens consist of large areas of wooden decking surrounded by lawns, bamboo and perhaps a few balls of box. These may offer places for small insects to nest, but are a very poor source of food for them.

This isn't just about pollen and nectar for bees, but about plants that contribute to all stages of the lives of many more insects: acting as host plants for larvae, and providing pollen and nectar for mature insects. Host plants are the very foundation of life around us. Butterflies and other insects lay their eggs on them so that the larvae can feed on their buds, leaves or fruit when they hatch. Lichen, fungi, beetles, wasps, butterflies: all are specialists in using their particular part of the host plant at specific stages of their development.

The foremost host plant in Sweden is the spruce, on which some 1,100 different species, 310 of them endangered, depend. But all native trees in any part of the world are important host plants, in contrast to imported varieties that have been lifted out of their ecological context and, as a rule, have no species attached to them when they are grown elsewhere. So it's time for the once classic spruce hedge to enjoy a renaissance!

Over hundreds of thousands of years, these native species have adapted to one another so that every tiny insect is dependent upon its plant. Sweden's national flower, the harebell (*Campanula rotundifolia*), has thrived in meadows and fields in the Nordic region since the dawn of time, and a large number of insects are dependent upon it; these include the scissor bee, which often spends the night inside the flowers. By contrast, the spreading bellflower (*C. patula*), which was imported into Sweden in the eighteenth century, still has no insect species associated with it, even after 250 years.

Such common plants as blackthorn, heather, goldenrod (*Solidago virgaurea*, not the invasive Canadian variety), yarrow and tansy are also important plants for insects in Sweden. Perhaps we will learn to love even nettles and thistles when we realize that they are host plants for some of our most beloved butterflies.

If we let wild, native plants into our gardens, we also encourage butterflies and other insects to visit. Everything is connected. Where there are caterpillars, there are chirruping birds, life and hope. But we need to find out more if we are to help insects thrive in our gardens. Through reading about butterflies, we learn, for instance, that the kidney vetch (*Anthyllis vulneraria*) is a host plant for the small blue butterfly. If we sow it in a sunny spot on poor soil, we can help our smallest blue butterfly to find our gardens and raise future generations. We also learn that the holly blue butterfly needs holly and ivy (*Ilex aquifolium* and *Hedera helix*) to reproduce, and so on, and this can inform the plants we use.

Traditionally, many parks have incorporated large areas of mown grass, which are as species-poor as any industrialized agricultural landscape. Gardens and parks in fact offer an opportunity to act as countermeasures in a landscape where biodiversity is under threat, offering endless chances to create habitats for birds, insects, bats, squirrels, frogs, newts and lizards. But it takes knowledge if we are to become aware of the requirements that can be crucial to the survival of these creatures that we live alongside. Planting native trees, such as willow, hazel, alder, birch, rowan, bird cherry, lime and maple, rather than exotic trees, has huge significance for biodiversity. Shallow water for reptiles, a sunny, sandy slope for solitary bees, piles of leaves for hedgehogs, an insect hotel – simple measures – can all have a big impact on biodiversity.

Today mown lawns are increasingly being turned into flower meadows, in whole or in part, in parks and gardens, and this is spreading across the country and the rest of Europe. But the planting of native species of trees and shrubs is not yet so common in urban environments.

All the garden and park designs in this book are based on the fact that it is entirely possible to combine biodiversity with aesthetic considerations. And everyone can contribute to this, whether you have a balcony or a garden, or live in a town or out in the countryside.

My favourites, many of them also loved by insects – as long as they aren't sprayed, of course

63° NORTH

My favourites for the north of the country, both on the coast and further inland.

BULBS

Allium, all forms
Crocus, all forms
Dwarf tulip (*Tulipa turkestanica*)
Glory-of-the-snow (*Scilla forbesii* syn. *Chionodoxa forbesii* 'Blue Giant')
Grape hyacinth (*Muscari armeniacum*)
Martagon lily, copper-coloured (*Lilium martagon* 'Orange Marmalade')
Martagon lily, white (*L. m.* 'Album')
Narcissus (*Narcissus poeticus* 'Actaea')
Narcissus, pure white (*N.* 'Thalia')
Siberian squill, blue (*Scilla sibirica*)
Siberian squill, white (*S. s.* 'Alba')
Snake's-head fritillary, white (*Fritillaria meleagris* 'Alba')

PERENNIALS, SPRING AND EARLY SUMMER

Lily-of-the-valley, white (*Convallaria majalis*)
Lungwort, dark blue (*Pulmonaria* 'Blue Ensign')
Oxlip, lemon-yellow (*Primula elatior*)
Pasque flower (*Pulsatilla vulgaris*)
Peony, pink, single (*Paeonia veitchii*)
Phlox, pale blue-violet (*Phlox divaricata* 'Clouds of Perfume')
Snowdrop anemone, white (*Anemone sylvestris*)
Speedwell, ice-blue (*Veronica gentianoides*)
Sweet rocket, white (*Hesperis matronalis* 'Alba')
Wood anemone, lavender-blue (*Anemone nemorosa* 'Robinsoniana')
Wood anemone, white (*A. n.* 'Vestal')

PERENNIALS, SUMMER

Amsonia, ice-blue (*Amsonia* 'Blue Ice')
Bleeding heart, white (*Dicentra formosa* 'Aurora')
Bowman's root (*Gillenia trifoliata*)
Catmint, violet-blue (*Nepeta* × *faassenii*, dwarf form 'Mini Walker' and tall 'Walker's Low')
Clary sage, deep violet, dark-stemmed (*Salvia nemorosa* 'Caradonna', dwarf form 'Caramia')
Corsican violet (*Viola corsica*)
Cow parsley, purple-leaved (*Anthriscus sylvestris* 'Ravenswing')
Daylily, yellow (*Hemerocallis lilioasphodelus*)
Fair maids of France, white (*Ranunculus aconitifolius* 'Flore Pleno')
Giant bellflower, white (*Campanula latifolia* var. *macrantha* 'Alba')
Giant cowslip, lemon-yellow (*Primula florindae*)
Globeflower, pale yellow (*Trollius* × *cultorum* 'Alabaster')
Granny's bonnet, sky-blue (*Aquilegia* 'Hensol Harebell')
Himalayan blue poppy (*Meconopsis baileyi,* syn. *betonicifolia*) [3]
Horned pansy, white (*Viola cornuta* 'Alba' and 'Minor')
Masterwort, white (*Astrantia major* 'Superstar', syn. 'White Giant')
Mullein, white (*Verbascum chaixii* 'Album')
Peony, single white (*Paeonia lactiflora* 'White Wings')
Perennial cornflower, white (*Centaurea montana* 'Alba')
Rosebay willowherb, white (*Epilobium angustifolium* 'Album')
Shasta daisy (*Leucanthemum superbum* 'Bröllopsgåvan')
Siberian iris, bright blue (*Iris sibirica* 'Caesar's Brother')
Siberian iris, white and pale blue (*Iris sibirica* 'Snow Queen' and 'Salute Ice Blue')
Spiked speedwell, blue (*Veronica spicata* 'Ulster Dwarf Blue')
Violet, lavender-blue (*Viola* × *williamsii* 'Belmont Blue')

PERENNIALS, LATE SUMMER

Astilbe, white (*Astilbe thunbergii* 'Professor van der Wielen')
Bugbane, white (*Actaea simplex* 'Brunette')
Daylily, pale yellow (*Hemerocallis citrina*)
Gentian, dark blue (*Gentiana makinoi* 'Royal Blue')
Heather (*Calluna vulgaris*)
Meadow rue, violet and white (*Thalictrum delavayi* 'Splendide' and 'Splendide White')
Menzies' burnet (*Sanguisorba menziesii*) [9]
Phlox (*Phlox paniculata* 'Rosa Pastell') [4]
Rue, violet/pale yellow (*Thalictrum* 'Elin')
Sea holly, violet (*Eryngium planum*)
Slender-leaved burnet, white (*Sanguisorba tenuifolia* var. 'Alba')
Speedwell, pink-white (*Veronicastrum virginicum* 'Album') [13]
Stonecrop, pink (*Hylotelephium* 'Matrona')

FERNS

Oriental wood fern (*Dryopteris orientalis*)
Sensitive fern (*Onoclea sensibilis*)
Shuttlecock fern (*Matteuccia struthiopteris*)

GRASSES

Feather reed grass (*Calamagrostis* × *acutiflora* 'Overdam')
Giant feather reed grass (*C.* × *a.* 'Karl Foerster')
Moor grass (*Sesleria nitida*)
Purple moor grass (*Molinia caerulea* 'Edith Dudszus')

1

2

3

4

5

6

7

8

9

FOLIAGE PLANTS

Barren strawberry, yellow-flowered (*Waldsteinia ternata*)
Dwarf lady's mantle (*Alchemilla erythropoda*)
Hazelwort (*Asarum europaeum*)
Hosta, green leaves with yellow margin, violet-flowered (*Hosta* 'Praying Hands')
Pearly everlasting, white (*Anaphalis triplinervis*)
Purple spurge (*Euphorbia dulcis* 'Chameleon')
Red barrenwort (*Epimedium × rubrum*)
Siberian bugloss, white-flowered (*Brunnera macrophylla* 'Betty Bowring')

SHRUBS AND TREES

Columnar Siberian crab apple (*Malus baccata* 'Columnaris')
Crab apple, white (*Malus toringo* var. *sargentii* 'Eskilstuna') [16]
Hazel (*Corylus avellana*) [2]
Japanese quince, red (*Chaenomeles japonica* cv. Motala E)
Japanese tree lilac (*Syringa reticulata* cv. Enskede E)
Lilac, lavender-blue (*S. vulgaris* 'Norrfjärden' E)
Manchurian cherry (*Prunus maackii* 'Honey' E)
Mock orange (*Philadelphus lewisii* var. *Gordonius* 'Waterton')
Modern shrub roses: white *Rosa* 'Louise Bugnet', pink *R.* 'Therese Bugnet'
Native rowan (*Sorbus aucuparia*) [8]
Panicled hydrangea, white (*Hydrangea paniculata* 'Great Star')
Scotch rose (*Rosa spinosissima* 'Plena')
Serviceberry (*Amelanchier laevis* cv. Bäcklösa E) [1]
Silver birch (*Betula verrucosa*) [7]
Willow (*Salix caprea*) [6]

HEDGING

Alpine currant (*Ribes alpinum* 'Öerne')
Crab apple (*Malus toringo* var. *sargentii* 'Eskilstuna')
Japanese spiraea (*Spiraea japonica* 'Waterer')
Norway spruce (*Picea abies* cv. Emmaboda)
Siberian larch (*Larix sibirica*)

CLIMBING PLANTS

Durand's clematis, dark blue (*Clematis durandii*) [5]
Regel's threewingnut (*Tripterygium regelii* 'Tiara' E)
Siberian clematis, white (*Clematis atragene* 'Riga' E)

55° NORTH

Supplementary favourites for central and southern Sweden.

PERENNIALS

Anemone, white (*Anemone* 'Ruffled Swan')
Aster, violet-blue (*Aster macrophyllus* 'Twilight')
Bearded iris (*Iris × germanica*)
Calamint, pale blue (*Calamintha nepeta* 'Blue Cloud') [18]
Coneflower, white (*Echinacea purpurea* 'White Swan')
Golden scabious, dark blue (*Scabiosa caucasica* 'Fama Deep Blue')
Hyssop, violet-blue, dark-stemmed (*Agastache* 'Black Adder')
Italian aster, dark blue (*Aster amellus* 'King George')
Japanese anemone, white (*Anemone × hybrida* 'Honorine Jobert') [15]
Lamb's ear, pink (*Stachys byzantina* 'Silver Carpet')
Lavender (*Lavandula angustifolia* 'Munstead')
Russian sage, blue (*Perovskia atriplicifolia*, dwarf form 'Little Spire' and tall 'Blue Spire')
Siberian iris, bright blue (*Iris sibirica* 'Silver Edge')

GRASSES

Japanese forest grass (*Hakonechloa macra*)
Korean feather reed grass (*Calamagrostis brachytricha*)
Purple moor grass (*Molinia arundinacea* 'Transparent')
Silver grass (*Miscanthus sinensis* 'Kleine Fontäne')

SHRUBS AND TREES

Carolina silverbell (*Halesia carolina*) [11]
Cornelian cherry (*Cornus mas*)
Crab apple, white (*Malus* 'Evereste')
Dogwood (*Cornus sanguinea* 'Winter Flame') [10]
Floribunda rose, white (*Rosa floribunda* 'Iceberg')
Hawthorn (*Crataegus × lavallei* 'Carrierei')
Japanese quince, white (*Chaenomeles japonica* 'Jet Tail')
Katsura (*Cercidiphyllum japonicum* cv. Göteborg E) [17]
Kentucky coffee tree (*Gymnocladus dioicus*)
Lilac, pale pink (*Syringa vulgaris* 'Beauty of Moscow')
Pearlbush, white (*Exochorda* 'The Bride')
Physocarpus (*Physocarpus opulifolius* 'Diable D'or')
Purple hazel (*Corylus avellana* 'Fuscorubra')
Sea buckthorn (*Hippophae rhamnoides* 'Hikul')
Seven-son flower (*Heptacodium miconioides*) [12]
Shrub rose, scarlet (*Rosa moyesii* 'Geranium') [14]
Shrub rose, whitish-pink (*R.* 'Champagne Wishes')
Smoke bush (*Cotinus coggygria* 'Royal Purple')
Spindle (*Euonymus planipes*)
Wedding-cake tree (*Cornus controversa*)
West Himalayan birch (*Betula utilis* var. *jacquemontii* [10]
Witch hazel (*Hamamelis × intermedia* 'Arnold Promise')

HEDGING

Common hornbeam (*Carpinus betulus* E)
Eastern hemlock (*Tsuga canadensis*)
European beech (*Fagus sylvatica* cv. Gottåsa)
Hybrid yew (*Taxus × media* 'Hillii')
Privet (*Ligustrum vulgare* var. *italicum* 'Atrovirens')

CLIMBING PLANTS

Clematis (*Clematis vitalba* 'Paul Farges')
Climbing hydrangea (*Hydrangea petiolaris*)
Giant Dutchman's pipe (*Aristolochia manchuriensis* E)

The numbers in square brackets refer to the photographs on pages 233 and 235.

10

11

12

13

14

15

16

17

18

Index of Plants

Page numbers in *italic* refer to captions.

Acknowledgements

I want to start by thanking all my clients, who over the years have given me something very precious: their trust in the creation of parks and gardens. It is a challenging and wonderful process in which artistic intent and technical solutions meet. My task is to take responsibility, to dare to see further than the wishes they have expressed, to listen and to bring plans to fruition, but the entire process requires the skill of many more people.

First I want to express my thanks to the landscape architects at Ramböll Stockholm who have worked on my projects over the years: Eva Pestmalis, Viktoria Wramsmyr-Ögren, Jessica Dahlman and Sara Pallin, to mention just a few.

Thank you, Björn Eriksen, for your digital treatments and constructive solutions; Anders Larsson for innovative solutions concerning ponds, fountains and calculations; Torbjörn Eliasson for your boundless enthusiasm for lighting so that we achieve the right result; and Christian Bjäråker for 3D images that help us all to understand what we have sketched out.

Thanks also to the manufacturers, such as Anders Löfven, Roger Olsson and Kenneth Posti at Svetsbolaget Conrad & Co., who convert my ideas into reality in steel and wood; and to Per-Anders Gustafsson at Naturstenskompaniet, who does the same in Scandinavian granite and slate. Thanks also to Bertils Stenarbeten, Rölunda Jord, Waterboys and the arborists of Peab.

I genuinely love all the plant nurseries, and Rainer Thomssen, Rosy Hardy, Mark Straver, Peter Clay and Mark Fane, Arnaud Boidin, Gunilla Nilsson and Richard Nordström, Michael Holmström and Carina Fredriksson, who are my guiding lights when it comes to plant production in Germany, the United Kingdom, France and Sweden. They all share the belief that nothing is impossible.

Thanks to Tolino Trädgård, and Tobias and Lisa Nordlund, who, together with their colleagues built the featured gardens in the Stockholm region in an innovative way and with great energy; to Jens Billing and Niclas Allsjö in Österlen; and to Franck Delmer's team and Giles Guenego, who did the same on the French Riviera. In Sweden, Ia Schildt, my working partner for the past twenty years, and her fantastic team have maintained and raised many of the gardens and terraces presented here to their current condition. Thanks to head gardener Elisabeth Häggkvist and her colleagues at Rydboholm Castle. Thanks to Mira Nilsson, who looks after Villa Norrnäs, and to all the council staff who maintain the parks in Lund and Umeå. Together, your ambition breaks new ground in gardening. With knowledge and experience, you hold everything together, from concept and construction to maintenance and development.

Jason Ingram's photographs work because they catch the feeling of each garden and the changes in the light. I am extremely proud of our collaboration, and I also want to thank Lisen Stibeck and Yanan Li, who have demonstrated in their pictures their own way of looking at gardens.

I am incredibly grateful to everyone in my network for their work on these projects. They are the reason this book exists at all. Hannu Sarenström, a friend of many years and my writing coach, has kept me on track and provided encouragement and input for which I am extremely grateful. Thank you to my editor, Malin Bergman, who with professionalism and patience has helped me and made sure my language is correct.

The Latin names have been checked by Björn Aldén, scientific officer at the Gothenburg Botanical Garden, and by Neil Smith, who also produced the English translation of the book; Karin Andersson fact-checked the chapter on Rydboholm Castle; and the landscape architect Thomas Lagerström (SLU/Ultuna) and Professor Jon Moen (SLU/Umeå) fact-checked the chapter on Change, with the input of Christel Kvant, who helped me to identify which species bees prefer.

The formatting, layout and graphic design of the book have taken me by surprise, and it has been a pleasure to work with the designer Elsa Wohlfahrt Larsson. Elsa has made a huge contribution to the character and identity of the book. Thank you to Tiina Henning-Wedemeier for turning my sketches into digital plans. Many thanks also to my publisher, Gunilla Bergmark, at Norstedts förlag, and to Elisabeth Douglas at Rydboholm Castle, who provided financial support for Jason Ingram's photographic work.

Finally, I want to thank the best thing in my life, Leif Häggkvist, who has supported and encouraged me when my courage failed, and my friends who have been with me all the way from Sweden, via London, to the French Riviera. Thank you for being there!

This book is dedicated to my mother, Alma Nordfjell (1906–1994), dearly loved and much missed. Her support still feels unconditional.

PUBLISHER'S ACKNOWLEDGEMENT

The publisher is grateful to the following sponsors for their generous financial support, without which the publication of this edition would not have been possible:

Johan Ahlberg
Elisabeth Douglas
Nils Tham
Hans Waldaeus

First published 2024 by Merrell Publishers Limited, London and New York

Merrell Publishers Limited, 70 Cowcross Street, London EC1M 6EJ

merrellpublishers.com

Neil Smith asserts his moral right to be identified as the translator of the work.

First published 2023 by Norstedts in Sweden as *Trädgårdar*
This edition published by agreement with Norstedts Agency

INSPIRATION Hannu Sarenström
DESIGNED BY Elsa Wohlfahrt Larsson
SKETCHES Ulf Nordfjell
DIGITIZED PLANS Tiina Henning-Wedemeier
nordfjellcollection.se

DESIGN ADAPTATION FOR ENGLISH EDITION Nicola Bailey
COPY-EDITING AND PROJECT MANAGEMENT Rosanna Fairhead
PROOFREADER Patricia Burgess

British Library Cataloguing-in-Publication data:
A catalogue record for this book is available from the British Library.

ISBN 978-1-8589-4719-8

Printed and bound in China

TIME

Nature teaches us that everything that grows is in a state of constant change over time – a concept that can be hard to relate to gardens and parks. The character provided by natural materials and neatly cut hedges and trees stands the test of time, while any experience of a garden varies according to how the light falls hour by hour, as well as by the growth and flowering of the garden. The art is to use a succession of plants to create change that enriches the garden. Through our choice of plants, we can change the garden's character and colour scheme from one month to the next. Change over the years takes more effort. As trees and shrubs develop, their volume, branch structure and bark become more beautiful, while also providing more shade and thus completely different growing conditions for the plants beneath. Root competition, and therefore drier growing areas, changes the nature of the planting. Almost everyone plants perennials too densely. Instead, plan for the bed to reach its peak in the third year, and divide and thin perennials in the fifth year. Perennials in groups have a greater impact than single plants. The challenge with time is that it passes without us noticing: after ten years trees dominate, bushes have grown large, and many perennials and bulbs have disappeared. The garden becomes at least in part a shade garden, a woodland with room for more shade-tolerant plants. Time plays with scale and proportions, so make use of this to allow the garden to develop. Do not hesitate to make changes whenever you feel like it, because the garden is yours for as long as you look after it.